Jeff

this book

blessing to you.

Ricardo

RICARDO GRAHAM

JESUS
UNLIMITED

Pacific Press®
Publishing Association

Nampa, Idaho | Oshawa, Ontario, Canada
www.pacificpress.com

Cover design by Steve Lanto
Cover art © Mark Missman. For more art from this and other artists, please visit
Sagebrush Fine Art & Licensing (www.sagebrushfineart.com)
Inside design by Kristin Hansen-Mellish

Copyright © 2014 by Pacific Press® Publishing Association
Printed in the United States of America
All rights reserved

Unless otherwise noted, scriptures are quoted from the King James Version of the
Bible.
Scripture quotations marked NASB are from the *New American Standard Bible*®,
copyright © 1960, 1962, 1963, 1968, 1971, 1972, 1973, 1975, 1977, 1995 by The
Lockman Foundation. Used by permission.
Scriptures credited to NIV are from the HOLY BIBLE, NEW INTERNATIONAL
VERSION®. Copyright © 1973, 1978, 1984 by International Bible Society, Inc. Used
by permission of Zondervan Publishing House. All rights reserved.
Scriptures quoted from NKJV are from The New King James Version, copyright ©
1979, 1980, 1982 by Thomas Nelson, Inc., Publishers.
Scripture quotations marked NLT are taken from the Holy Bible, New Living
Translation, copyright © 1996. Used by permission of Tyndale House Publishers,
Inc., Wheaton, Illinois 60189. All rights reserved.
Scriptures quoted from RSV are from the Revised Standard Version of the Bible,
copyright © 1946, 1952, 1971 by the Division of Christian Education of the National
Council of the Churches of Christ in the U.S.A. Used by permission.

The author assumes full responsibility for the accuracy of all facts and quotations as
cited in this book.

You can obtain additional copies of this book by calling toll-free
1-800-765-6955 or by visiting http://www.adventistbookcenter.com.

Library of Congress Cataloging-in-Publication Data:

Graham, Ricardo, 1950– author.
  Jesus unlimited / Ricardo Graham.
     pages cm
  ISBN 13: 978-0-8163-5611-9 (hard cover)—ISBN 10: 0-8163-5611-4 (hard cover)
  1. Jesus Christ Biblical teaching.—Person and offices 2. Jesus Christ—Person
and offices—Meditations. I. Title.
  BT203.G725 2014
  232—dc23
                                   2014029314

September 2014

Dedication

To my loving wife, without whose encouragement this book never would have been written.

Contents

Chapter 1

Jesus: The Way, the Truth, and the Life

P eople used to name their children after a prominent family member or some character trait they valued. Now they pick names that sound good or are in vogue. Popular singer Beyoncé and rapper Jay-Z (Shawn Carter), for instance, named their daughter Blue Ivy Carter.

Sometimes, names that top the popularity polls even make the news! A couple years ago, CNN reported that the Parent.com name search Web site said the top five names for girls were Isabella, Millie, Sookie, Ann, and Ella—Isabella being the most popular. The top five names for boys were Jacob, Max, Liam, Ted, and Mo.

A friend of mine named his sons Dwight and Calvin. When I asked him whether he had named them for the deceased United States presidents Dwight Eisenhower and Calvin Coolidge, he said No. He'd given them the names of two people he respected deeply—but they weren't political figures; they were long-departed Christian ministers: the theologian and Reformer John Calvin and the great preacher Dwight L. Moody.

I've met people whose names are actually titles: Mister and Queenie and even Major. When black people were deliberately shown disrespect in public—grown men being called "boy" and women "gal"—they gave names like this to their children, hoping to evoke a measure of respect for them.

Jesus—the great I AM

On many notable occasions, God instructed earthly parents what to name their children. For instance, He told Abraham what to name his son of promise, a forebear of Jesus. "God said, Sarah thy wife shall bear thee a son indeed; and thou shalt call his name Isaac: and I will establish my covenant with him for an everlasting covenant, *and* with his seed after him" (Genesis 17:19). And more than a thousand years later, God sent an angel to tell Zacharias what to name his son, the forerunner of the Messiah: "Thou shalt call his name John" (Luke 1:13).

And when it came to naming the Savior, God was particular. He didn't use an Internet search engine to decide on a name for this very special baby yet unborn—this child of promise, the earth's eternal Redeemer who was preexistent, but who was now coming into the world shrouded in flesh. Through an angelic messenger, the eternal Father told Joseph: "Thou shalt call his name *Jesus:* for he shall save his people from their sins" (Matthew 1:21; emphasis added).

According to the apostle Paul, Jesus is the eternal God. In Paul's letter to the Colossians, he says of Jesus: "He is the image of the invisible God, the firstborn over all creation. For by Him all things were created that are in heaven and that are on earth, visible and invisible, whether thrones or dominions or principalities or powers. All things were created through Him and for Him. And He is before all things, and in Him all things consist" (Colossians 1:15–17, NKJV). John 1:1–3 says the same thing about Jesus: "In the beginning was the Word, and the Word was with God, and the Word was God. . . . All things were made by him, and without him was not any thing made that was made."

One source comments on the meaning of Jesus' being the "image" of God.

Jesus was an "exact likeness" of God—a "perfect Representative."

> Christ . . . perfectly reflected visibly "the invisible God" (1 Ti 1:17). . . . "Likeness" implies mere *resemblance,* not the exact *counterpart* and *derivation* as "image" expresses; hence it is nowhere applied to the Son, while "image" is here, compare 1 Co 11:7 [TRENCH]. (Jn 1:18; 14:9; 2 Co 4:4; 1 Ti 3:16; Heb 1:3). Even before His incarnation He was the image of the invisible God, as the Word (Jn 1:1–3) by whom God created the worlds, and by whom God appeared to the patriarchs. Thus His *essential* character as *always* "the image of God," (1) before the incarnation, (2) in the days of His flesh, and (3) now in His glorified state, is, I think, contemplated here by the verb "is."[1]

If this is true, and it is, then Jesus undeniably is the God who called Moses to deliver the Hebrew slaves from their Egyptian bondage. When Moses asked the God of eternity what he should call Him, God said, " 'I AM WHO I AM.'* Just tell them, 'I AM has sent me to you' " (Exodus 3:14, NLT).

Notice that Jesus said He bears that name. He declared of Himself, "I am the way, the truth, and the life" (John 14:6, NKJV). When He said, "I am," He repeated His introduction of Himself to Moses. *I AM* is a form of the verb *to be,* so Jesus introduced Himself as the One who is. This statement implies that He is the eternal, self-existent One. No one else gave Him life or in any other way brought Him into existence. Like the Father and the Holy Spirit, Jesus is eternal. He therefore exists above and beyond time and circumstances. Because He is above and beyond human time and circumstances and thus isn't limited or controlled by them, He can *interrupt, intercede, intersect,* and *interpret* times and circumstances for us.

And because He is above and beyond them, He can also *infiltrate* them. Because He is always and at all times "I AM," He always *is*. He ever lives. Because He always *is,* every day is always today and not yesterday or tomorrow. He is Jesus Christ, *"the same yesterday,* and *to day,* and *for ever"* (Hebrews 13:8; emphasis added).

God *knows* all about our cares and sorrows because He is ever present with us.

And God *cares* for us.

Therefore God *appears* whenever His people need Him.

And God *provides* whatever His people need.

---

*   Or I Will Be What I Will Be.

The Way

Just before His trial and crucifixion, Jesus told Thomas, "I am the way, the truth, and the life. No one can come to the Father except through Me" (John 14:6, NLT). In other words, He was saying that *He is the only road* that takes travelers to the Father.

Our spiritual journey is a journey of faith. It is designed to take us into the fullness of fellowship with the Father. But this journey doesn't begin with Southwest Airlines or Amtrak or Greyhound. It doesn't start at an airport. It begins in our hearts and minds. It is a journey to a place inside that will take us to a place outside. It is a journey not of place and time but a journey of our being. It is a journey of our becoming.

You see, we have been separated from God by our sinfulness. "Your iniquities have separated you from your God, and your sins have hid His face from you, so that He will not hear" (Isaiah 59:2, NKJV). This sinfulness has affected our very being and nature. Our journey of faith is designed to re-create in us the nature that Adam and Eve lost for all of us in the Garden of Eden—and to re-create the relationship that also was lost in that garden. It is a journey in which we are restored to the image and nature of God, first in our character and then in our bodies. It is our own fallen nature that cultivates within us the desire to do the evil that we do. We need a way back to God—a road back to Him. This way, this road, is Jesus.

Have you ever noticed that some streets and roads are faulty? They may be poorly identified or too narrow or unpaved and muddy. The way to God isn't like that. It's clearly mapped out, in good repair, and free of hindrances. But that doesn't mean that it's level and easy to travel. It has its hills and valleys, its sharp curves. But it's a true road, and it leads upward to everlasting life.

Jesus said, "Enter ye in at the strait gate: for wide is the gate, and broad is the way, that leadeth to destruction, and many there be which go in thereat: Because strait is the gate, and narrow is the way, which leadeth unto life, and few there be that find it" (Matthew 7:13, 14). This road is the clear way. While it is invisible to the world, it is visible to the eye of faith; it is visible to believers. It makes itself manifest in the lives of those who have found it.

Jesus is also the way from earth to heaven. He is the way from sin to purity. He is the way from wrong to right. He is the way from death to life. He is the way from ignorance to enlightenment. He is the way from weakness to strength. He is the Way of all ways.

The Bible informs us that some people have already traveled this road successfully: Enoch, Moses, and Elijah the Tishbite. Enoch was pure and holy in a world drowning in sin. Moses, who could have been a pharaoh, gave his life to leading God's people to the Promised Land. And Elijah stood for God when it seemed he was the only one still faithful.

But even these three people needed a mediator between themselves and God. That Mediator was, is, and ever will be Jesus. Paul wrote, "There is one God, and one mediator between God and men, the man Christ Jesus" (1 Timothy 2:5).

Ellen White pictured this in another way. She said, "Christ is the way from earth to heaven. By His humanity He touches earth, and by His divinity He touches heaven. He is the ladder that connects earth and heaven. . . . Because of His incarnation and death, 'a new and living way' has been consecrated for us (Heb. 10:20). There is no other means of salvation (Acts 4:12; 1 Tim. 2:5)."[2]

It is Jesus who is the Great Way-Maker. Have you ever needed someone to make a way for you, to—like a blocker in a football game—run interference for you and thereby clear a path for your feet? Jesus has done this for all of us. Because He is the great I AM, He has credibility with God, with Satan, with all the other angels, fallen and unfallen. They all respect Him. Consequently, when He mediates with God for us, the issue is settled. When He commands Satan on our behalf, the issue is likewise settled—all because Jesus is the great and mighty I AM, the eternal Way-Maker.

The Truth

Jesus is also the Truth. He is the absolute Truth, the full Truth, the only Truth, the eternal Truth. He is nothing but the truth. The *Seventh-day Adventist Bible Commentary* notes, "In its basic meaning truth is that which corresponds to fact. John frequently, as here, uses the word in a wider sense to denote what is true in things pertaining to God and the duties of man, or in a more restricted sense the facts taught in the Christian religion concerning God and the execution of His purposes through Christ."[3]

There can be no truth without Jesus. Philosophers may philosophize, strategists may strategize, debaters may debate,

quibblers may quibble, but without Jesus and His Word enter-
ing in, all is false and untruthful. *It is Jesus who determines truth,
because there is no reality without Him.*

A common teaching of our age is *relativism.* Its adherents
believe there is no eternal, changeless truth. What is true var-
ies with a person's life situation. What is true for me may not
be true for you. All things are relative to a person's thinking,
desire, goals, and so forth.

Jesus undercuts that teaching by declaring that He is the
standard by which all lives are to be judged. Therefore, He is
the *objective* truth, not the *subjective* truth. His principles are
universal and timeless, and His teachings are applicable to all
humanity.

Being the Truth means living the truth and telling the
truth. And from the beginning, Jesus has been truthful with
humanity.

Jesus told Adam and Eve that they would surely die if they
ate the forbidden fruit.

Lucifer, through his artful ventriloquism using the serpent,
said that they would *not* surely die. Adam and Eve believed the
devil's lie—and we've been dying ever since!

Here's the truth as it is in Jesus:

> The only way in which men will be able to stand
> firm in the conflict, is to be rooted and grounded in
> Christ. They must receive the truth as it is in Jesus. And
> it is only as the truth is presented thus that it can meet
> the wants of the soul. The preaching of Christ cruci-
> fied, Christ our righteousness, is what satisfies the soul's

hunger. When we secure the interest of the people in this great central truth, faith and hope and courage come to the heart. If God has given his Son to die for sinners, he means to counteract sin. He has made the great gift because of his love for sinful, fallen man. We must make it plain that he is able and willing to save all who come unto him and believe in him as their personal Saviour. Present this again and again, until the mind can take it in. Let every teacher put his whole heart, his whole mind and soul, into this work, lifting up Jesus, and bidding the people look and live. Let the sinner fix his eyes on Jesus, the Lamb of God that taketh away the sin of the world. As he looks to Christ, he will feel the power of God. He must not devote the precious time to deploring his sinfulness, looking upon the wounds and bruises he has received in the services of Satan. By faith carry the mind up within the veil to view Christ as our intercessor before the mercy seat. Let the sinner behold Jesus as the way, the truth, and the life, and his soul will be open to receive the truth as it is in Jesus.[4]

Because Jesus is the unvarnished truth, He calls us to live lives that are truthful, truth filled, and truth bound. He is the "naked" truth.

I once heard a story in which truth and lies were personified to draw a stark contrast between the two. Long ago and far away, Truth and Lie lived in the same little town. Truth was always dressed in white from head to toe. He wore a white hat, a white shirt, a white suit with a white tie, and white socks and shoes. He was always meticulous in his dress. Lie, on the other hand, was always filthy.

Truth was out for a walk one hot day, and he came upon a lake. Since it was the time of day when no one else was likely to come there, he decided to go skinny-dipping. He hung his clothes on some shrubs and low-hanging tree branches with care, making sure nothing would fall off nature's clotheslines onto the ground. Then he slipped into the pristine waters of the lake and swam away.

About that time, Lie happened to come along. He noticed the immaculately clean clothing hanging on the shrubs and tree branches, and a nefarious idea came to him. He quickly slid out of his filthy clothes and exchanged them with the pristine ones that belonged to Truth. Then, disguised as Truth, Lie walked back to the town and began to deceive people.

After a while, though, someone shouted, "Here comes the real Truth!" Then, as the people of the town peered into the distance, someone asked, "How do you know that is the real Truth and not an impostor?"

The answer came back, "Because it is the naked Truth!"

Truth refused to wear Lie's filthy clothing.

Jesus is like that. He never appears in the filthy clothes of falsehood. He *is* the truth, and He *reveals* the truth. When He spoke the Ten Commandments from Mount Sinai, He spoke and then wrote truth. We must obey the Ten Commandments—every last one of them—for they are truth, having come from the mouth of the Lord and then being written by His finger. Aligning ourselves with the truth of the universe—the truth of God and His righteousness—is always the best policy. He is the one and only True Witness—the witness to the eternal truth of the Godhead. And in His revelation of truth, He is not general but specific:

> And unto the angel of the church of the Laodiceans write; These things saith the Amen, the faithful and true witness, the beginning of the creation of God; I know thy works, that thou art neither cold nor hot: I would thou wert cold or hot. So then, because thou art lukewarm, and neither cold nor hot, I will spue thee out of my mouth. Because thou sayest, I am rich, and increased with goods, and have need of nothing; and knowest not that thou art wretched, and miserable, and poor, and blind, and naked: I counsel thee to buy of me gold tried in the fire, that thou mayest be rich; and white raiment, that thou mayest be clothed, and that the shame of thy nakedness do not appear; and anoint thine eyes with eyesalve, that thou mayest see. As many as I love, I rebuke and chasten: be zealous therefore, and repent (Revelation 3:14–19).

As the holy Healer of eternity past, present, and future, Dr. Jesus tells us the truth about our spiritual condition—and about our diagnosis and prognosis. The diagnosis defines our ailments, our disease, our real condition. It is the act or process of identifying or determining the nature and cause of a disease. Through the prophet Isaiah, God asks His people, "Why should ye be stricken any more? ye will revolt more and more: the whole head is sick, and the whole heart faint" (Isaiah 1:5).

The prognosis is a prediction of the probable course and

outcome of a disease—the likelihood of recovery. So the Lord calls us: "Come now, and let us reason together, saith the LORD: though your sins be as scarlet, they shall be as white as snow; though they be red like crimson, they shall be as wool. If ye be willing and obedient, ye shall eat the good of the land: But if ye refuse and rebel, ye shall be devoured with the sword: for the mouth of the LORD hath spoken it" (Isaiah 1:18–20).

Yes, Jesus is the Truth, the whole Truth, and nothing but the Truth!

The Life

When Jesus says He is the life, He is telling us several things. First, He is saying that no life exists without Him. We took a look at John 1:1–3 a few pages back and saw that it portrays Jesus as the Creator-Redeemer. Paul wrote in a similar vein: "By him were all things created, that are in heaven, and that are in earth, visible and invisible, whether they be thrones, or dominions, or principalities, or powers: all things were created by him, and for him" (Colossians 1:16).

According to the Bible, then, God—Jesus—made the world in six literal days, and then He rested the seventh day and blessed it and hallowed it. And His creative activities continue. We are alive today because of Jesus. He made us, and He sustains us. "In him we live, and move, and have our being" (Acts 17:28).

But more important, Jesus is the model human being. His life is the supreme example of what the Father wants the lives of all of us to be like. We are to live our lives after the simil-itude, the likeness, of Jesus' life. He, who was pure and holy, demonstrates and models before us how to be holy. Without this holiness, we will not see God. Jesus said, "Blessed are the pure in heart, for they shall see God" (Matthew 5:8). And Paul wrote, "Follow peace with all men, and holiness, without which no man shall see the Lord" (Hebrews 12:14).

Jesus is the definition of a holy life, the presentation of a holy life, and the power that enables us to live a holy life. It is Jesus in us and us in Jesus that results in eternal, everlasting life.

"God would make known what is the riches of the glory of this mystery among the Gentiles; which is Christ in you, the hope of glory" (Colossians 1:27). The only hope we have is the hope of Christ living out His life within ours as we surrender to Him.

We aren't really living until we live the life that Jesus has set before us. We live the life of Jesus through the Holy Spirit living in us and producing the righteous results of that indwelling in our lives.

Once again, Paul speaks clearly about the "fruit"—the results—of the indwelling of Jesus in us through the person of the Holy Spirit: "The fruit of the Spirit is love, joy, peace, long-suffering, kindness, goodness, faithfulness, gentleness, self-control. Against such there is no law" (Galatians 5:22, 23, NKJV).

There are many ways of determining whether or not the tree that's being examined is an apple tree. Expert arborists can distinguish the different varieties of trees by examining their bark, branches, root system, and leaves. But the easiest way to know what kind of tree we have is to look at the fruit it produces. After all, Jesus did say, "By their fruits you will know them" (Matthew 7:20, NKJV).

Of course, Jesus wasn't really concerned with trees. He was saying we know whether or not people are Christians—followers of Christ—when we see whether or not they have the "fruit of the Spirit" in their lives.

Does this mean that if we don't have all the fruits of the Spirit, then we aren't Christians? No. While these fruits will be manifested completely in the people who surrender themselves to God daily, we must remember that we are "under construction." God is, through His divine operations, growing Christians. He is making us more and more Christlike daily. And He is in charge of the total operation; we are not. We are the willing subjects of His work, and we share the responsibility for the work—we must cooperate with Him. But ultimately, the credit and the glory will all be His.

When we come into a salvific relationship with Jesus, God judges us by looking at Jesus. He accepts the merits of His life in place of the selfishness, sin, and disobedience in ours.

He was unselfish, so we are to become unselfish.

He was loving, so we are to become loving.

He was kind, so we are to become kind.

He was patient, so we are to become patient.

He was temperate, so we are to become temperate.

He was joyous, so we are to become joyful.

He was obedient, so we are to obey.

Little Timmy's punishment

Years ago in a small rural town, there was a group of students no teacher had been able to handle. They'd even managed to run off three teachers in a single school year.

A young man just out of college heard about the class, and he applied to the school. In the pre-employment interview, the principal warned him, "You don't know what you're asking for. No one has been able to handle these students. You're likely to be beaten terribly."

After a few moments of silent prayer, the young man looked at the principal and said, "Sir, I want to take on the challenge. Just hire me on a trial basis."

The next morning the young man stood before the class and said, "I'm here today to teach you—to help you learn. But I realize I can't run the school by myself. I need your help."

A boy whom the local people called Big Tom was sitting in a desk at the back of the room. He whispered to his buddies, "I don't need any help. I can lick that little bird all by myself!"

The teacher told the kids that if they were to have a school, there'd have to be some rules. But then he said that they'd be the ones to make up the rules; he'd just write them on the blackboard.

The students were surprised. This teacher's way of conducting school certainly was different!

The students began to suggest rules. One said, "No stealing," and someone else shouted, "Be on time for class," and thus it continued till ten rules were listed on the board.

The teacher then asked the class what consequences there should be for breaking these rules. "Rules don't do any good unless they're enforced," he said.

One of the students suggested that all those who broke one of the rules be given ten licks across their back with a

rod. The teacher thought that was pretty harsh, so he asked
the kids if they would stand by this punishment. They all said
they would.

Everything went pretty well for two or three days. Then
at lunchtime, Big Tom came in very upset. He said someone
had stolen his lunch.

Someone said he had seen little Timmy holding Big Tom's
lunch. So the teacher called little Timmy to the front of the
room, and he soon admitted that he had taken Big Tom's lunch.

Then the teacher asked little Timmy, "Do you know what
the punishment for stealing is?"

Little Timmy nodded. He knew what it was.

"You'll have to take off your coat," the teacher said. Little
Timmy was wearing a great big coat.

Timmy pleaded, "I'm guilty, and I'm willing to take my
punishment. Please don't make me take off my coat."

The teacher reminded little Timmy of the rules and pun-
ishments and again told him he must take off his coat and take
his punishment like a man.

The little fellow started to unbutton his old coat. As he did
so, the teacher saw that he wasn't wearing a shirt under the
coat. He also saw little Timmy's frail, bony frame, which he'd
obviously wanted to keep hidden beneath that old coat.

The teacher asked Timmy why he had come to school
without a shirt on. Timmy replied, "My daddy's dead, and
we're very poor. I don't have but one shirt, and my mother is
washing it today. I wore my big brother's coat so's to keep warm."

The teacher looked at the frail back with the ribs and the
spine practically pushing themselves through Timmy's skin.

He wondered how he could lay a rod on the little back that didn't even have the slight protection a shirt would provide. Yet, he knew he must enforce the punishment or the children would no longer obey the rules. So he raised the rod to strike the first blow.

At that, Big Tom stood up and came down the aisle, asking, "Is there anything that says I can't take little Timmy's whipping for him?" The teacher thought about it and said No. Then Big Tom ripped his coat off and stooped over little Timmy, who still lay on the desk; and hesitantly, the teacher began to ply the rod on Tom's big back. But for some strange reason, after only five licks, the rod broke in half.

The young teacher buried his face in his hands and began to sob. Then, hearing a commotion, he looked around the room and saw that all the students were crying too. Little Timmy turned, threw his arms around Big Tom's neck, apologized for stealing his lunch, and begged for his forgiveness. He told Big Tom that he would love him till the day he died for taking his whipping for him.

Jesus, the Creator of heaven and earth, came as was prophesied to show us the way, to teach us the truth, and to give us eternal life. He took the punishment that we deserve so we can live with Him throughout eternity.

Aren't you glad that He loves us!

Endnotes

1.   Colossians 1:15, in R. Jamieson, A. R. Fausset, and D. Brown, *Commentary Critical and Explanatory on the Whole Bible* (Oak Harbor, WA: Logos Research Systems, Inc., 1997).

2.   Francis D. Nichol, ed., *The Seventh-day Adventist Bible Commentary* (Washington, DC: Review and Herald®, 1980), 5:1035.

3.   Ibid., 5:989.

4.   Ellen G. White, *General Conference Daily Bulletin,* January 28, 1893.

Jesus and His Message

J esus was preparing His disciples for His crucifixion and departure. He was about to leave His
fledgling group—those to whom He was en-
trusting His church. So He gave them a final lecture.

It was the summation of all He had demonstrated in His
great galactic show-and-tell. He reminded them of the focus
of His ministry. John, the beloved apostle, recorded it in these
words: "So now I am giving you a new commandment: Love
each other. Just as I have loved you, you should love each
other. Your love for one another will prove to the world that
you are My disciples" (John 13:34, 35, NLT).

A new commandment

Jesus plainly stated that He was delivering a new commandment to His disciples. He was giving them the responsibility of building on the foundation that He laid during the
three short, intense years of His ministry.

This new commandment wasn't crystalized in words at
the beginning of His ministry, but throughout those three and

a half years of modeling and teaching, the essence of the commandment was fleshed out before them. The definitive statement of it came near the end of our Lord's ministry.

This commandment can be understood as being just as weighty, just as authoritative as the Ten Commandments, which Jesus, as God, spoke to the newly coalescing nation of Israel and then wrote with His own fiery finger in stone tablets on Mount Sinai, which He then entrusted to Moses to deliver to the Israelites.

So, what is this "new thing" that Jesus, the Master Teacher, the righteous Rabbi, was presenting to His disciples of old? And what does it mean for us who are living in the twenty-first century?

The essence of the commandment is love. It may seem strange to think of love as something that can be commanded. I think it obvious that Jesus isn't talking about love as a feeling. Feelings cannot be commanded. No one can control how another person feels about a particular issue or experience.

It may be argued that people can't predetermine how they feel about an issue or an experience—that they can react to it only as they are actually experiencing it or as they are re-experiencing it via their memories. Our feelings are *subjective*—subject to the impact of previous experiences that were similar or at least had an effect similar to the experience in question.

Remember, a subjective idea is one that is based on opinions or feelings rather than on facts or evidence. Someone has said that opinions are like noses—everybody has one. In our self-focused society, we are very subjective. Most people have an orientation that makes them see everything in terms of "me, my, and mine."

Our subjectivity is taken to the extreme when we move to the point of relativism, which makes everything, every choice, relative to our situation. In relativism, our personal choices and desires are the ground from which all our decisions grow. We have no external standard by which to guide our behavior or lifestyle. Everything is relative to what we want to do, which usually is based on our feelings. We are the masters of our own destiny, the captains of our own ships, the centers of the universes in which we live. Personal preference controls our every decision. It, rather than principle, is the foundation of our self-government.

The objective, on the other hand, is based on facts rather than the varying feelings, thoughts, and opinions of the people involved. Objectivity takes us above and beyond our personal desires and wants. It can lead us to the realization that the laws that operate the universe are in effect in our individual lives as well.

Jesus' command to love is objective. In other words, it is based on principle. A principle is a fundamental truth or proposition that serves as the foundation of a system of belief or behavior or of a line of reasoning.

Principle versus preference

Sometimes we mistake our operational parameters and proceed to operate on the basis of preference rather than principle. Let me illustrate.

I understand that to gain and to maintain health, I must include green vegetables in my diet. Now, there are a plethora of green vegetables that I can eat to apply the principle to my dietary experience. I don't have to eat green peas every day or at all. I can eat broccoli, turnip greens, spinach, okra, cabbage, asparagus, and more while both applying the principle and simultaneously satisfying my preference. It is when I exclude *all* green vegetables from my diet that I reject the principle and, at least in the long run, damage my physical health.

As Christians, we must let principle rather than preference control the decisions we make. We are safe only when we direct our choices, our lives, based on the principles of God, and we can safely satisfy our preferences only as they stand within the shelter of the principles God has made known to us for our good. To ignore this is to place ourselves outside of God's plan.

God gave a version of this nearly all-encompassing commandment to Israel of old. He told His people: "Never seek revenge or bear a grudge against anyone, *but love your neighbor as yourself. I am the LORD*" (Leviticus 19:18, NLT; emphasis added). This statement is obviously the basis for Christ's command in Matthew 22:39. (This may make you ask, If ancient Israel received this command in the time of Moses, then why did Jesus say, nearly a thousand years later, that it was a new commandment? I'll get to that in a moment. First, let's finish the other part of this discussion.)

In Matthew 22:37, Jesus ranks the commandment to love God supremely as the greatest commandment of all time. And then He says that our obligation to love other people comes in as a close second. Apparently, nothing else ranks with these two.

Jesus also taught that all of the Ten Commandments "hang"—in other words, *depend*—on love. Thus, Jesus defines love as the foundation of our relationship with God and other human beings.

In Matthew 5:44, He tells us to love our enemies and to bless those who curse us, to do good to them that hate us, and to pray for those who despitefully use us. Tall order, isn't it?

Jesus repeated the subject of love because we need to hear it again and again. There is something about our fallen condition, our sinful, selfish hearts, that necessitates our hearing the voice of Jesus again and again urging—encouraging—us to emulate Him. "Repetition deepens impression" as they say, and the lifestyle of Jesus revealed the principle of love over and over again.

And we like to hear the word *new*.

On his first Sabbath with the congregation he had just agreed to pastor, the minister delivered a wonderful message on love. Everyone thanked him for the great sermon.

The next Sabbath, the minister preached the very same sermon. While the congregation still thought the sermon to be a good one, they wondered why the minister was repeating himself.

When the minister delivered the same sermon on his third Sabbath there, the members sent a delegation to inquire of him the reason for the repetition. "Pastor," the elders said, "we appreciate your sermon on love, but don't you have anything new to preach?"

The pastor replied, "You haven't learned that lesson yet. Why should I move on to something else?"

While this little story may or may not be factual, it makes a good point. We, as the disciples of Christ, need to have the message repeated to us until we learn it. Whether or not we have learned the lesson will be demonstrated by whether we practice the values we have heard from Jesus and have gleaned from His Word.

Back to "new"

Now, back to the question regarding what Jesus meant when He called the commandment He gave His disciples a *new* one. First, Jesus was modeling for His disciples the love He was saying they should have. He said, "As I have loved you, . . . you also [are to] love one another" (John 13:34, NKJV).

Jesus was modeling what He was asking His disciples to do, and the model that He was living was expanding His disciples' understanding of love's range of operation and of what it meant to actually apply that principle in every aspect of their lives. The powerful fact is not that Jesus commands us to love and tells us that love is the essence and core of His kingdom. The powerful fact is that He *demonstrated* His unselfish love continuously and unconditionally in His daily life.

For instance, Jesus said we are to love our enemies. What Jesus did demonstrated that this wasn't merely abstract ideology. Rather, the way Jesus lived showed the disciples how love works—what it does. Jesus didn't follow the "do as I say, not as I do" principle. He practiced the "do as I say *and as you see me do*" principle. Jesus loved *all* His disciples—including Judas, the one who betrayed Him with a kiss.

Second, this commandment is new in that in it Jesus tells *us* to love as He loves—with the expectation that this is within the realm of possibility for us. Jesus "did" as He taught. It has often been said, particularly about the academic or scholarly community, "Those who can't, teach." In other words, it is alleged that those who can't practice a particular craft choose to teach the very skills that they themselves have failed to master. While I don't particularly subscribe to this critique of the teaching community, I do believe that Jesus demonstrated the principle of all-inclusive love by living it before all those around Him.

Third, this commandment is new because Jesus alone has perfectly demonstrated what true love is as a principle of action. Prior to His coming, this love idea was poorly demonstrated. There was no one who could show perfectly in the flesh what true agape love was all about. I'm sure that some came close. I think of Enoch, who lived so close to God that God literally lifted him out of this world.

Jesus took flesh like ours upon Himself and gave a perfect demonstration. How did He love? *Completely, fully, unconditionally, and without limitation or reservation.* Jesus didn't limit His love to Jews only. He loved all people—Jews and Gentiles, males and females, saints and sinners. Think of how He treated the Syrophoenician woman, and the ten lepers, and the woman caught in the act of adultery.

All of these examples and more broadcast across the ages that the message of Jesus is unconditional, unlimited, unrestricted love! That is because when true love, divine love, is the principle that motivates what we do, we don't give it only to those who are like us—those who are of the same ethnicity or culture. Jesus' love operates above and beyond these small, satanically inspired confines.

When we love as Jesus loves, we transcend the barriers of gender, race, education, position, and so forth that Satan has raised to separate the human family, and we learn to love all people everywhere.

Jesus didn't love just the "good" people. He spent His time with the sinners. The one accurate accusation that His critics leveled against Him was, "This Man *receives sinners* and eats with them" (Luke 15:2, NKJV; emphasis added). Jesus didn't associate with sinners so He could do what they did; He associated with them because He loved them and He wanted to show them how much God values them.

Jesus did receive sinners. He promised, "Those the Father has given me will come to me, and I will never reject them" (John 6:37, NLT).

Jesus didn't throw out the castoffs of society. He accepted all people because He lived by God's terms, not by those of humanity. He lived freely—He wasn't concerned about the criticism He would receive for doing what was godly.

Jesus demonstrated His love—His agape love—by accepting sinners, by helping suffering humanity, and by living a totally unselfish life.

Jesus demonstrated the highest order of love—agape love. This kind of love is what is spoken of here. It is of the *sacrificial* variety. It is *totally unselfish* in its nature. It is a love that gives. And that is exactly what God is calling us to do—to live unselfishly with each other.

The play *Pygmalion* contains the line "You can give without loving, but you cannot love without giving." That is why Jesus gave. He loved as His Father—our Father—loves. John 3:16 states clearly the connection between love and giving:

"God so loved the world that He gave His only begotten Son, that whoever believes in Him should not perish but have everlasting life" (NKJV).

A soldier who was stationed in Vietnam during the war there became intimately involved with a young woman during his tour of duty. Upon returning to the United States, though, he returned to his high school sweetheart and eventually they married.

Soon after the wedding the soldier learned that his liaison with the young Vietnamese woman had resulted in the birth of a child. Smitten by guilt, he decided to bring the child to America to raise her in the land of the free and the home of the brave. Amazingly, his wife agreed to help him find the child and adopt her.

They did find the child, but while they were in the process of adopting her, the former soldier was found to have an inoperable, incurable form of cancer. He died without fulfilling the dream.

But the story doesn't end there. The soldier's wife, motivated by love for her deceased husband, completed the adoption and brought his child to her home to give her the advantages she would have in this country.

And, incredibly, the soldier's widow also sponsored the immigration of the child's mother and then invited her to live with her.

What a wonderful story of the power of love!

However, the greatest love story ever told is that of the innocent Jesus. He was arrested on false charges, beaten unmercifully, and insulted by Herod's request that in the midst of all that He was suffering, He perform a miracle! (See Luke 23:8.) And all this was merely the preliminaries. Ultimately, Jesus died on the rugged timbers of Calvary's cruel cross—because of His love for us.

Now this Suffering Servant tells us that we are to love each other as He has loved us. His love was sincere, and it was real. It wasn't fake or false. The apostle John wrote, "He that loveth not knoweth not God; for God is love" (1 John 4:8).

Love in action says more clearly than anything else that we know God.

Sign of discipleship

Jesus emphatically stated that love, agape love, is the irrefutable sign of discipleship. Love is universal. It works in every part of the world—in every society, among all people. I believe that as people see the love that exists among Jesus' modern-day disciples, they recognize that this is something other than what humans can produce. They realize who the Master is. They see this love as evidence that God is at work there.

People should be able to get some idea of what the leader of a religious faith is like by observing those who claim to be that person's devotees. Disciples are walking advertisements of their master's work. There may be some flaws in the product, but generally speaking, you should learn something about a master by examining his or her teachings and their effects on the disciples, the devotees.

The only true source of the love Jesus said we should have is God the Holy Spirit. As we are involved in a spiritual love relationship with Jesus, He reproduces this love in our hearts and minds. Our souls become citadels that lovingly accept all of humanity.

I am convinced that this is a supernatural experience that is induced by God the Holy Spirit only while we submit to Him—the One who leads us into the fullness of righteousness. "Love is the basis of godliness. Whatever the profession, no man has pure love to God unless he has unselfish love for his brother. . . . When self is merged in Christ, love springs forth spontaneously."[1]

As we seek Christ, we develop a love for others. We must merge with Christ, letting Him take ascendancy, authority, and rulership for our souls. We must deny self and seek Him.

The apostle Paul understood the need to deny self. He wrote, "I affirm, by the boasting in you which I have in Christ Jesus our Lord, I die daily" (1 Corinthians 15:31, NKJV). In order for godly agape love to exist, self must die, and it must do so on a daily basis. We must surrender through prayer and intentional thought.

We surrender through exposing ourselves to the presence of the Holy Spirit. We die by choosing to serve rather than to be served.

Self dies hard. In fact, it must be executed. If we will avoid withholding ourselves from God, He will make new men and new women of us—men and women who love as He does.

The message that Christ brought to this world is the message of God's great love for fallen humanity. That message has been obscured.

It is the darkness of misapprehension of God that is enshrouding the world. Men are losing their knowledge of His character. It has been misunderstood and misinterpreted. At this time a message from God is to be proclaimed, a message illuminating in its influence and saving in its power. His character is to be made known. Into the darkness of the world is to be shed the light of His glory, the light of His goodness, mercy, and truth. . . .

. . . The last rays of merciful light, the last message of mercy to be given to the world, is a revelation of His character of love.[2]

Let us live lovingly among those around us so that we may give glory to God. And let us practice self-denial that love may grow.

Endnotes

1.   Ellen G. White, *Christ's Object Lessons* (Mountain View, CA: Pacific Press®, 1941), 384.
2.   Ibid., 415.

Chapter 3

Jesus and His Mission

Living as a man, as a human being while He was on earth, Jesus submitted to the Holy Spirit. Thus He was filled with the Holy Spirit, and that Spirit inspired Him to define His mission scripturally.

Since Jesus and His disciples were united in a single spiritual organism—Jesus, the head, and His disciples, the body—the mission that was Jesus' was also the mission of His church. It's our mission too. We're to do what He did when He lived on earth. We're to follow His example, to take His life as our pattern.

In Luke 4:18, Jesus presented Isaiah 61:1 as the scriptural blueprint of His mission: "The Spirit of the Lord is upon me, because he hath anointed me to preach the gospel to the poor; he hath sent me to heal the brokenhearted, to preach deliverance to the captives, and recovering of sight to the blind, to set at liberty them that are bruised."

Jesus was anointed and appointed.

He was deputized and set aside.

He was elected and selected for the work of God.

Jesus' ministry was to grow out of His anointing, and it

was to be multifaceted. His ministry was people-focused and God-centered. God always directs the work of saving the lost.

To preach the gospel to the poor

In this scripture, the first group of people that Jesus identifies as the focus of His ministry is the poor.

Few people want to be poor. Very few volunteer to live in poverty. Most of us desire to be rich, or at least to be "comfortable." But Jesus was poor. He was homeless. He owned only one set of clothing and one pair of shoes.

Jesus wasn't poor because of laziness—the reason some are poor today. He was poor because He *chose* to be poor. He chose to identify Himself with the impoverished people of this planet; the poor in all ages. He could have come as the wealthiest of all, but He came poor.

In this world the poor usually are plagued by bad health and low self-esteem. They live in substandard housing. Many live near or in "bad neighborhoods," where they are disenfranchised and more vulnerable to the criminal element than are other classes of our society. Often, those who are well off take advantage of them, disrespecting, mistreating, and vilifying them. They don't consider them to be important. And rather than treating them as fellow beings who, like them, bear God's image, they "tolerate" them and "allow" them to exist.

The first item in Jesus' list of assignments was ministry to the poor. Jesus has a preference for the poor—not because He is a respecter of people but because of their need. People who know their need and who admit it are more receptive to the gospel message than are those who think themselves to be rich and in need of nothing.

The poor also have less of the diversions of this world—less of the things that block people's vision of the gospel.

Jesus wants us to help the poor. "When the nations are gathered before Him, there will be but two classes, and their eternal destiny will be determined by what they have done or neglected to do for Him in the person of the poor and the suffering."[1]

The gospel says the poor will have an inheritance in Christ equal to that of the cultured, the educated, and the wealthy, for God is no respecter of persons. In fact, Jesus said that it is the poor in spirit who will be given the kingdom of heaven. (See Matthew 5:3.) The poor can find joy and encouragement in the knowledge that the gospel of Jesus Christ makes them just as acceptable and worthy of the kingdom as are those who have more of this world's goods. Through it they receive the power they need to live well despite their poverty.

But it's not only in the world made new that the poor will experience the material blessings of God. Over the years of my ministry I have observed many times that people who were living in poverty when they became Adventists experience a change in their financial situation. The biblical message has an uplifting power about it income-wise as well as spiritually. I have seen people join the church with nothing and then, inspired by the gospel, find a new determination to do more and be more; to rise above their appointed lot through sacrifice and industry. And as they focus on Jesus, they are blessed with a measure of prosperity.

Some remain poor, but Jesus still takes care of them, and they find that joy in Jesus is better than money in the wallet—for when they accept the gospel and they accept the Christ of the gospel, they realize that they are children of the heavenly Father.

There are worse things than being poor.

To heal the brokenhearted

Jesus came not only to preach the gospel to the poor but also to "heal the brokenhearted"—or, as a literal translation might put it, He came to heal those whose hearts have been crushed.

Many things can crush our hearts. A romance that has gone bad. A promotion that we were all pumped up about but didn't get. Seeing our youth reject all that they have learned and seen in God's house and choose the world instead.

Some of us have hearts that sin has broken and crushed to smithereens. We have done evil things, and now we are burdened with guilt because Satan's agents remind us in glaring detail of our fallenness.

Jesus said that part of His mission is to heal the brokenhearted; to bind up those hearts that are bruised and bleeding.

Is your heart broken?

When Jesus hung on Calvary's cross, a Roman soldier pierced His heart with a spear. When he did, blood mingled with water poured from his riven side, indicating that His heart had burst before that spear thrust. Jesus died of a broken heart. So, we have the assurance that Jesus knows how to help us, because He knows what it is to have a broken heart. He has experienced it Himself.

Jesus' heart is crushed whenever He sees His children embrace sin. It is crushed every time we choose a night of television or the movies when we haven't spent any time at all with Him. And yet Jesus is the heavenly Healer. Christ the divine Cardiologist is the only one who can bring joy to the joyless. He alone can cheer the grieving and the depressed. Only He can teach the sorrowing how to live again and to love again.

Are you suffering physical pain, discouragement, rejection, or persecution? Jesus knows! He understands, because He Himself has felt the pain of rejection. He's been through it all.

Yes, He knows how to heal our hearts. His very presence brings peace and comfort to those who accept Him.

And never before was this healing ministry needed more than it is now. There are people all around us who are hurting. They come to church dressed up and smiling—hiding the pain they're feeling inside. They carry burdens that we cannot see, and they bleed with blood we cannot see.

They need the touch of Jesus. We must direct them to Him.

To preach deliverance to the captives

Jesus came also to preach deliverance to the captives. He wasn't talking about releasing our loved ones from prison. Yes, there are many who are incarcerated without a cause; yet it is not the mission of Jesus to set them free.

Sam Tannyhill was convicted of first-degree murder in Fremont, Ohio. Keith Collins and another member of the Seventh-day Adventist Church went to visit him. They asked him if he would read a Bible if they brought one to him. Sam said Yes. They brought him the Bible that belonged to Keith's nine-year-old son. That moved Sam.

Sam read the Bible from his perspective as a criminal. When he read that Jesus borrowed a donkey for the triumphal entry into Jerusalem, he concluded that Jesus was a horse thief. When he read that Jesus turned water into wine, he thought Jesus was a bootlegger. However, as Sam read the Bible and prayed, the Holy Spirit worked on his heart, and he was converted and eventually baptized. But even though Sam gave his heart to Jesus, he was executed.

No, Jesus wasn't talking about the freeing of those who are in prison because they have committed crimes. He was talking about what the gospel does for those held captive by their sins. Every sinner is a captive of the devil. In fact, the word *captive* is basically a military term meaning "one taken in war."

We are fighting a war. It is not a literal war, but it is a real war. "Though we walk in the flesh, we do not war after the flesh: (For the weapons of our warfare are not carnal, but mighty through God to the pulling down of strong holds)" (2 Corinthians 10:3, 4).

Paul called Timothy to enlist in this battle: "This charge I commit to you, Timothy, my son, in accordance with the prophetic utterances which pointed to you, that inspired by them you may wage the good warfare" (1 Timothy 1:18, RSV).

In this warfare for the souls of men and women, we are fighting the devil and his fallen angels. "We wrestle not against flesh and blood, but against principalities, against powers, against the rulers of the darkness of this world, against spiritual wickedness in high places. Wherefore take unto you the whole armour of God, that ye may be able to withstand in the evil day, and having done all, to stand" (Ephesians 6:12, 13).

Sometimes in the battles of this war, the enemy takes captives. The sinners are captive to Satan. Some of us are the devil's POWs: prisoners of war. Some of us are MIAs: people who have gone missing in action. Satan, God's enemy, doesn't recognize the Geneva Convention articles of war. He wants to kill us by any means possible—to destroy us bit by bit or all at once.

Many of us are languishing in the prison house of sin. Many are chained to the wall of immorality, serving a sentence because of our sexual sinfulness.

No human being can escape from the devil. He grants no pardons. He gives no paroles from his captivity. He will never grant anyone release of any kind for good behavior. He holds fast the captives he has won in the battles, and he wants to hold them—to hold us—till we roast in hell's fire with him.

Jesus, on the other hand, releases us. He gives us liberty. He sets the captive free.

He proclaims it. He states it. And when He says something, it is a fact. What He says He will do, He does.

What Jesus does for those held captive by sin is a reality that is sometimes beyond our belief. He declares us free and at liberty, and the same voice that created the world by speaking sets us free by speaking. Jesus' word is powerful, and at His command we are set free.

Jesus, sweet Jesus, has come to preach deliverance to the captives.

No matter what we have done that has allowed the devil

to take us captive, Jesus can deliver us. His blood breaks down the kingdom of Satan brick by brick.

You see, Jesus left heaven on a rescue mission. He has infiltrated the enemy's stronghold. He has dropped behind enemy lines, and He will break us out of our captivity and deliver us to freedom.

On Calvary, He dealt the devil a mighty blow from which he will never recover. On Calvary, Jesus gained our spiritual freedom. Through His death and resurrection He has gained our deliverance. Oh, what a wonderful Savior!

To preach recovery of sight to the blind

Then there are the blind. While on earth Jesus opened the blind eyes of many, but here He's talking about spiritual blindness. Jesus warned us of this blindness. He said we're so blind that we say, I am rich, I have prospered, and I need nothing; not knowing that we are wretched, pitiable, poor, blind, and naked (see Revelation 3:17).

Our spiritual condition of blindness has left us destitute, wretched, poor, miserable, and naked, and we don't know our true condition. Without Jesus, we live in darkness. But He will come to give us spiritual insight and to open our eyes to see Him in all of His wonder and beauty.

"To set at liberty them that are bruised"

Jesus came to set at liberty those who are bruised. Just looking at the people around us, we can see that there are many in this world whose lives sin has broken—has shattered. Many are living under Satan's oppression.

When sin comes to us, it brings with itself guilt and shame. These oppress us. They hold us down, and we can even develop clinical depression because of our sin.

The compassionate Christ was also oppressed and broken by sin—not by His sins, but by ours. But the *tragedy* He suffered on the cross becomes a *triumph* for all who will accept Him. All who are in Christ Jesus are set at liberty. The oppressed go free!

Yes, Jesus came to preach the gospel to the poor, to heal the brokenhearted, to preach deliverance to the captives and recovering of sight to the blind, and to set at liberty those who are oppressed. He came to make us His children—children of the king. As the old hymn says,

> My father is rich in houses and lands;
> He holdeth the wealth of the world in his hands!
> Of rubies and diamonds, of silver and gold,
> His coffers are full—He has riches untold.
>
> I'm a child of the King, a child of the King!
> With Jesus, my Savior, I'm a child of the King!
>
> My Father's own Son, the Savior of men,
> Once wandered on earth as the poorest of them;
> But now He is pleading for sinners on high,
> And will give me a home when He comes by and by.

I'm a child of the King, a child of the King!
With Jesus, my Savior, I'm a child of the King!

I once was an outcast, a stranger on earth,
A sinner by choice, and an alien by birth!
But I've been adopted, my name's written down,
An heir to a mansion, a robe, and a crown.

I'm a child of the King, a child of the King!
With Jesus, my Savior, I'm a child of the King!

A tent or a cottage, O why should I care?
They are building a palace for me over there!
Though exiled from home, yet still I may sing:
"All glory to God, I'm a child of the King."

I'm a child of the King, a child of the King!
With Jesus, my Savior, I'm a child of the King!

—Hattie E. Buel

Our Father knows just how much we can bear.

Endnote

1.   Ellen G. White, *The Desire of Ages* (Mountain View, CA: Pacific Press®, 1940),
      637.

Chapter 4

Jesus and His Ministry

Jesus' message and His mission were reflected in His ministry. Ministry is nothing more and nothing less than service. For the Christian, it is both spiritual and practical in nature.

Jesus set a high tone for service when He stated, "The Son of man also came not to be ministered unto, but to minister, and to give his life a ransom for many" (Mark 10:45). In saying this, Jesus was defining His ministry, His service, as being other-directed. "Self-serve" didn't fit His model. He came to serve others. He didn't come to take; He came to give.

It often seems as though the self-serving are highly rewarded in this world. Those who "get theirs" seem to be on the top of the heap. Not so with Jesus. He wasn't self-centered. He was totally unselfish. His focus was on doing the will of the Father—your Father and mine. He came as God's personal ambassador to represent what God the Father is truly like.

The thought that Jesus, the Son of man and the only begotten Son of God, would leave the place where holy angels worshiped Him and come to this world to serve nasty human beings seems impossible. Yet that is exactly what He did. In coming to this earth, the great God of heaven stooped low to lift us high. The Creator served the creatures He had created.

In all that Jesus did during His short public ministry, which lasted about three and a half years, He ministered to the needs of humanity. All the miracles He performed were done to meet the needs of others. For instance, when He was attending a wedding, His mother told him that the wedding party had run out of wine. This was a crisis that posed the possibility of extreme embarrassment for the family. Imagine inviting people to a wedding and not having enough food to serve them! If we had been guests there, we might have accused the family of planning poorly.

Jesus didn't do that. After consulting with His mother, He simply ordered the servants to fill some large jars with water. When they did, the water was instantaneously transformed into wine. What's more, the wine He produced was of a better quality than the wine they'd been serving. (See John 2:1–11.) Jesus, the Servant-Savior, cared. He demonstrated that nothing was too small for our God to attend to.

The Bible says Jesus fed large multitudes (Matthew 14:14–21). He felt sorry for the people who had come to hear Him, and so, out of compassion, He provided food for them to eat. He didn't send for "take-out," nor did He go on a shopping trip. He took what little was available and prayed to the God of heaven, and then He began to feed the crowd. The Bible states that He provided for them in abundance—there was so much food that there were leftovers. Jesus met people's needs because He is loving, merciful, and caring.

Many Bible expositors believe that every miracle Jesus

performed served two purposes. They all gave glory to God the Father, and they all demonstrated that Jesus was indeed the Son of God in human flesh. His miracles of feeding the hungry, healing the sick, and raising the dead presented the truth about God, correcting the characterization of the religious establishment of Jesus' day, which didn't understand that God is love.

Other forms of service

Jesus' teaching and preaching ministry was also a significant form of service. The truths He taught people were powerful and life-transforming. Jesus said truth liberates us—it sets us free. When we have God's truth operating in our lives and we are following God's principles, we are free indeed.

Jesus also served by giving hope to the hopeless and joy to the sad. He served them by cheering those who thought they had nothing to be cheerful about. And He served downtrodden, guilt-burdened sinners when He forgave their sins. In doing so, He was lifting them out of their sinfulness.

Jesus is still serving today. His main office is no longer found in the dusty streets and roads of Palestine. He has relocated it to heaven, but He still serves people on earth. He still makes house calls. He's come to my house when I was heavyhearted and downtrodden, and I'm sure He's been to yours as well.

Jesus has sent His true representative, the Holy Spirit, the Comforter, to earth. This God without flesh can simultaneously reach every heart, mind, and soul in this world and fill

all of us with the joy, cheer, and forgiveness we need. The Holy
Spirit brings to us the fresh power of Jesus to help us meet the
needs of this life.

Jesus' supreme ministry was His giving of His life as a ransom for sinners. His blood shed on Golgotha's cross provided
for our salvation. Jesus, the only innocent Person who ever
lived on this planet, died in your place and mine. After living
a life of service to God and to humanity, He was executed in
our place. In rising from the grave, He has given us the victory
He gained over sin, Satan, and death. His Holy Spirit living
in us gives us both the desire and the power to obey His will.

The implications

What are the implications to us today of Jesus' life of service? First, we live with the understanding that His life of
service is focused on us. He served so that we could have
the gift of eternal life. His death, burial, and resurrection earn
for us what we never could earn for ourselves and do not
deserve—eternal life. It is through Jesus' sacrifice that we are
cleansed and kept holy enough to live with God forever. It is
not by our works but by faith in His works that we enter into
the kingdom. It is not works but a love-driven faith that draws
from us willing obedience to His commands.

Second, as His disciples we must pattern our lives after
His. We must follow His example and serve God and our fellow human beings. We may not be able to heal the sick, but
we can alleviate suffering. We can visit the sick and shut-in
and let them know that they are not forgotten. We can tutor

young people and give them the tools they need to be better students. We can share out of our abundance to help the poor all around us here and in foreign lands.

Once, while I was pastoring a church in the Midwest, I conducted a series of meetings to introduce people to Jesus and some of the forgotten truths of the Bible. An elderly woman dependent upon a walker came to the meetings.

At the end of the service one night, she told me she wanted to join our church. I said she didn't know what we believed well enough yet to take that step. But she kept insisting that she did know enough.

So, I decided I would visit her in her home. There, she told me that a young married couple in our church had befriended her and helped her by taking her grocery shopping and to medical appointments, and they had even cleaned her house! They showed her their compassion and caring by serving her—by meeting her needs. Their unselfishness touched her heart, and she gave herself to Jesus because of it.

When we look at all Jesus has done for us, the only response anywhere near to adequate is to give ourselves to Him and to join Him in serving others. The only question that remains is, How can I serve today?

Chapter 5

The Mind of Jesus

A song that was popular in the 1960s boldly proclaimed, "It's your thing, do what you wanna do." It was practically the mantra for those who were growing up in that turbulent decade. The idea of living a self-focused, self-pleasing life wasn't new, but the music gave it an extra push—bringing the "do your own thing" maxim of that decade to life.

That maxim is still alive, and it's as representative of our times as it was of those five decades ago. The self-help gurus of today—well, most of them, anyway—tell us that if we want to find happiness and success, we have to give top priority to taking care of ourselves. And many of these teachers tell us that if we do serve others, it's really only because of the WIIFM factor—that is, the "what's in it for me?" factor.

The names of the programs change through the years. The promoters try to disguise what they're selling by calling it self-fulfillment, self-affirmation, or similar positive-sounding things. But the core of all these philosophies is experiencing as much pleasure as we can. Many people see this as more than a quest. They regard it as a right—a moral or legal entitlement.

After all, the United States' Declaration of Independence states that Americans have certain "unalienable rights," among which is "the pursuit of happiness."

Jesus set an entirely different example for us. Paul said that Jesus was "in the form of God, [and He] thought it not robbery to be equal with God: But [He] made himself of no reputation, and took upon him the form of a servant, and was made in the likeness of men. And being found in fashion as a man, he humbled himself, and became obedient unto death, even the death of the cross" (Philippians 2:6–8).

The biblical documentation is clear: Jesus didn't cling to or fight for His "right" of being God. Instead, He, in humility, gave up this right so that He could free us from our sins. Jesus Christ freely forfeited the right He had of being equal with God and became instead a servant.

Whom did He serve?

First and foremost, He served the Father—carrying out the will of Someone with whom He was a full equal. He submitted Himself to the will of the divine Mind, living in fallen flesh as a man fully surrendered to God. Day in and day out, hour by hour, and moment by moment He lived to please the Father and to do the Father's will. And during His ministry, He—the Anointed One—repeatedly stated that He had come to fulfill His Father's desires, not His own (see John 5:19, 20; 8:15, 16, 28, 42; 14:10).

Jesus wasn't focused on doing His own thing. He surrendered His will to the Father, and—if you will allow me to coin a phrase—He did "God's thing," not His own.

A brief examination reveals that Jesus lived a life of utter and complete self-denial. Contrary to what some people are proclaiming through various media outlets today, Jesus never married or fathered children—which certainly has been the right of all other human beings. Nor did He amass a fortune or gather a political following. He just lived out what He taught when He said, "If any man will come after me, let him deny himself, and take up his cross daily, and follow me" (Luke 9:23).

Jesus lived to obey His Father. Nowhere can there be found a single record of a misdeed or sin that Jesus committed. He was so fully focused on doing the Father's will that when Philip asked Him to show him the Father, Jesus could reply, "He that hath seen me hath seen the Father" (John 14:9). Jesus' character was a mirror image of His Father's character. He yielded Himself so completely to the Father that He could say with humble confidence—not boastfully—that He was the embodiment of God. What He said and what He did revealed God's will for all human beings.

Jesus' submission to the will of the Father was so complete that He embraced His divine destiny—which was to be "the Lamb of God, which taketh away the sin of the world" by becoming the sacrifice, the offering on the cross of Calvary (John 1:29).

Second, Jesus not only served God; He served people too. He was "other" focused—He paid more attention to helping and healing other people than to meeting His own needs. The corrupt spiritual leaders of His day accused Him of all sorts of misdeeds. But the only accusation they made against Him that had an element of truth to it is recorded in Luke 15:2: "The Pharisees and scribes murmured, saying, This man receiveth sinners, and eateth with them."

Yes, Jesus received sinners then, and He receives them now. He fulfills the will of God by receiving us, taking us in, accepting us just as we are, and applying His powerful blood to us when we repent. He not only receives us sinners, but He also pardons us and empowers us to "go and sin no more" (John 8:11).

I'm glad that Jesus receives sinners, because I need Him to receive me.

A servant mentality

Jesus serves all because He has a servant mentality—an attitude of meekness and humility. What does this have to do with us? To the Philippians, Paul wrote, "Let this mind be in you, which was also in Christ Jesus" (Philippians 2:5). Paul told them, and he tells us, that we are to have the mind—the mindset or attitude—of Jesus. He tells us to let the mind of Jesus be in us.

In other words, we are to allow Jesus' mind to enter into us, to become ours.

How does this happen? By the power of choice—by our choosing to be one with God, and by our allowing God the Holy Spirit to reproduce this attitude in us today.

Someone has said that human beings are "free moral agents." God has given us the power of choice; the power to decide, the power to choose or refuse, to accept or reject. Our Father won't ignore our power to choose because He won't violate our will. Though often our decisions are unrighteous, He regards them as valid and doesn't try to overturn them by force. He will woo us with love and compassion, but He will never force us to follow Him or to obey Him.

The Holy Spirit will dwell in us if we invite Him into our lives. He will then reproduce in us the servant mentality—the humility and meekness—of Jesus. As a result, it will be our highest joy to serve God and other people.

To be humble is to be meek or modest in behavior, attitude, or spirit. To turn away from our arrogance and pride. Humility and meekness go hand in hand.

How do we know whether we are experiencing the mind of Christ in humility and meekness?

Those who ride horses use a bit, bridle, and reins to control them. Years ago, I read that a horse that takes easily to the bit, bridle, and reins—a horse that is easily led—is called a meeked horse.

Have we become "meeked people"? How easy is it for God to lead us? The true sign of humble followers of Christ is that they yield easily to His call. They are easy for Him to lead. They gladly follow His directions.

The opposite of being meek is being *stiff-necked*—a term God used throughout the Old Testament to describe rebellious Israel. It's hard to turn a horse that stiffens its neck when its rider signals that it's time to turn.

Meekness is not weakness. It is an attitude of teachableness —of having a teachable spirit. It is the willingness to listen to and consider what God is saying, and then to accept it as being in our best interest.

Jesus was humble. He demonstrated His humility by stooping down to raise us up. He wrapped His divine nature in fallen flesh and came to this dark, sin-filled earth. He was born in a barn and laid in a manger. The Creator of all the gold and silver, silk and linen in the world grew up as a member of the working class. He had no worldly wealth. He didn't own a house, or a horse, or a mule.

Jesus wasn't self-promoting. He wasn't proud and arrogant. He was meek and lowly. He stayed close to His Father and was quick to follow His lead. And He was obedient even though His obedience took Him to a torturous death on a cross, where He suffered and died, not for His own sin and guilt but for ours. His death was the greatest demonstration of meekness and humility that could be given.

We have a decision to make. The song says we can make our lives be all about our thing—our pleasure, our satisfaction, ourselves. We can choose that, or we can follow where God leads. That's in our best interest anyway, because He wants to bring us to our heavenly home. We choose to let Him do that by saying, "Yes, Lord," to each of His commands.

Chapter 6

Jesus, the Champion

When I was a child, our family visited my maternal grandparents quite frequently. Sometimes when we visited them on a Friday night, my granddaddy would watch the Friday night fights on TV and simultaneously listen on the radio to the preaching of Pastor C. L. Franklin, pastor of the New Bethel Baptist Church in Detroit, and yes, Aretha Franklin's father.

TV on, sound off; radio on, sound up—an interesting mix indeed!

These memories came to mind as I read an article about a popular athlete who left home at the age of fifteen, seeking a better life. He'd grown up in a family of eight who lived in a country gripped in deep poverty. He often shared his meager meal with people who were even hungrier than he was.

This man learned to fight when he was living on the streets. He liked fighting and decided to become a professional pugilist—a boxer.*

Known for his aggressiveness, his lightning-fast hands, and

---

* Don't take my inclusion of this story in this book as an endorsement of boxing. I don't watch that sport or mixed martial arts. I'm writing about this man to make a point.

his powerful punches, he has, in the opinion of many, mastered the style of boxing that emphasizes offense and often renders opponents helpless.

Arguably the most exciting boxer since Muhammad Ali, Emmanuel "Manny" Dapidran Pacquiao has conquered seven weight divisions in his thirty-one years. Many people consider him to be a champion and a hero.

There have been a lot of sports champions through the years. I think of—in the United States—Joe Louis, Jackie Robinson, Babe Ruth, Jack Nicklaus, Michael Jordan, Bobby Orr, Joe Montana, Willie Mays, Hank Aaron, Mickey Mantle, Reggie Jackson, Rafer Johnson, Johnny Weissmuller, Wilma Rudolph, LeBron James, Kobe Bryant, and Steve Nash. We may have second thoughts about giving a blanket endorsement to the lifestyles of all or any of them, but we cannot ignore or gainsay their contributions to the sport of their choosing.

Take Colin Kaepernick for instance. He began his pro career as the San Francisco 49ers' backup quarterback to starter Alex Smith. When Smith was injured in the middle of the 2012 season, Kaepernick filled in for him, becoming the full-time starter as the 49ers advanced to the National Football League (NFL) play-offs for the second straight season.

In Kaepernick's first play-off game, he set an NFL record for most rushing yards by a quarterback in a single game—either regular season or play-offs, running for 181 yards. After beating the Atlanta Falcons in the National Football Conference Championship game by a score of 28–24, he led the 49ers to their first Super Bowl appearance since 1994.

And how about Serena and Venus Williams, the two young women out of Compton, California, who have reshaped tennis history forever? Venus Williams is *a seven-time* Grand Slam title winner (singles), and Serena Williams is a *seventeen-time* Grand Slam title winner (singles)! Both of these women were coached from an early age by their parents, Richard Williams and Oracene Price.

There is a rivalry between them—when this chapter was written, they had met as opponents in eight Grand Slam singles finals—yet they have a very close relationship. Often, when one sister has been eliminated from a tournament, she will stay in support of her sister.

As of this writing, Serena is the U.S. Open champion again—for the fifth time. On September 9, 2013, she beat a relentless Victoria Azarenka 7–5, 6–7 (6–8), 6–1 for her seventeenth Grand Slam singles title. She is just one win behind Chris Evert and Martina Navratilova on the all-time list.

The Bible's champions

The Bible has its champions too. We think of David defeating Goliath and of Gideon vanquishing the far more numerous Philistine marauders with just three hundred Israelite soldiers. Of course, there's also Samson, who, as a blind, fallen, enslaved Israelite warrior, took out more Philistines by his sabotage of a crowded building than he had in all his preceding years.

Joshua, on God's command, marched the Israelites around the walls of the besieged city Jericho every day for a week. Then, on the seventh day, when the trumpets blasted the sound of victory and the people added their shouts, the walls came "tumbling down."

The Bible certainly has other heroes of faith too. Many of them are named in chapter 11 of the book of Hebrews. There's Moses, and David, and we must not forget Deborah or Queen Esther, who, despite the possibility of bringing a death sentence upon herself, entered the king's chamber without invitation, saying, "If I perish, I perish."

Despite the fame all these champions have earned, though, the day is coming when they will have to "bend the knee" with the rest of humanity to the all-time, undisputed, universal Hero and only true Champion, Jesus Christ.

My dictionary gives two definitions for the word *champion*. The first is "a person who has defeated or surpassed all rivals in a competition, especially in sports." The second is "a person who fights or argues for a cause or on behalf of someone else."

Jesus fits the bill on both counts. He has beaten the devil in His own defense, and He fights the foe for us!

Yes, Jesus is God's Champion. He is heaven's Champion. And He is our Champion—the Champion for the entire human race.

In a familiar passage in Paul's letter to the Philippians, the apostle tells us a few things about our universal Champion and Hero. Paul says that He,

> being in the form of God, thought it not robbery to be equal with God: but [He] made himself of no reputation, and took upon him the form of a servant, and was made in the likeness of men: And being

found in fashion as a man, he humbled himself, and became obedient unto death, even the death of the cross. Wherefore God also hath highly exalted him, and given him a name which is above every name: That at the name of Jesus every knee should bow, of things in heaven, and things in earth, and things under the earth; And that every tongue should confess that Jesus Christ *is* Lord, to the glory of God the Father (Philippians 2:6–11).

Jesus was humble.

Imagine saying that about the Creator of the universe and all that dwells in it! But it's true: only a humble being would obey someone else—particularly when he knows that his obedience will result in his death and that he won't die as an innocent being who's been mistakenly condemned but as a criminal who's been tried and convicted. And infinitely worse, He will die without the certainty of a resurrection and eternal life.

But Jesus chose to obey, and His obedience brought Him victory, which in turn has brought Him the adoration and adulation—the worship—of the world.

What in particular did Jesus conquer?

He conquered His own humanity. He came in the flesh He inherited as a son of His human mother—flesh that came with all the weaknesses that human beings have. Yet He conquered.

He conquered cheating, lying, and stealing—all forms of dishonesty. Jesus was continuously, completely honest.

He conquered sexual impurity. Yes, if it is true that there is
nothing new under the sun, some form of pornography, some
temptations to lust existed in His day, and He conquered them.

He conquered idolatry in every form. He refused to bow
to the gods of this world—not only the wooden, stone, and
metal gods made by human hands but also the gods of popularity, materialism, and the like.

Jesus said No to other "isms" too—to classism, racism, sexism,
ageism, and more. Jesus loved all people and considered them all
equally valuable. He deliberately broke the social and religious
taboos of the day, demonstrating by His actions that God loves all
people and offers forgiveness and salvation to all people.

Jesus broke down all sorts of barriers to talk with the
woman He met at a well in Samaria. She was a Samaritan and
He a Jew, but He shattered the wall of racial discrimination to
talk with her.

She was a woman, yet Jesus considered her as worthy of
salvation as the men with whom He spoke, thus destroying
the wall of gender exclusiveness.

Her religious beliefs and practices differed from His, but
He rejected the idea that she was to be avoided because of that.

She was an unescorted woman, and He hadn't been for-
mally introduced to her, yet He considered her salvation of
more importance than the social mores of that time and place.

And she was a serial adulteress, yet Jesus didn't consider her
so lost in sin as to be beyond redemption.

Jesus broke all the taboos of His day to reach a person who
needed His ministry.

Jesus conquered the sins of political corruption and

bribery, misrepresentation and misuse of Scripture, and pandering to people who could benefit Him. He resisted all these temptations and overcame them all.

Perhaps most impressive, He conquered His ego—the source of the sins of self-centeredness and self-promotion. Ellen White indicated how difficult and how important that is. She wrote, "The warfare against self is the greatest battle that was ever fought."[1]

Jesus stooped to full and complete self-abnegation and died the death of a sinner for us so that we might be made righteous through faith in Him. He has conquered the enemy of our souls, Satan. He has conquered the grave, sin, death, and hell. He has conquered all!

And not only has He conquered sin for Himself, He also has conquered it for all humanity—and more than that, for the whole universe!

So, yes, Jesus is a Champion.

Jesus became sin for us when He willingly accepted our sins and bore them to Calvary. Paul told the Corinthians, "He hath made him to be sin for us, who knew no sin; that we might be made the righteousness of God in him" (2 Corinthians 5:21). In other words, Jesus has set up a kind of spiritual exchange. We give Him our impurity, and He gives us His purity. We give Him our sinfulness, and He gives us His righteousness.

His taking on of our sins wasn't something He did easily. It was *heavy*, as they say. And what He did wasn't simply metaphorical or symbolic or allegorical. It was real. It was the mysterious working of God.

We must understand that Jesus is the purest of the pure,

the most righteous of all Creation, the only holy Son of God, the original Mr. Clean. Thousands upon thousands of angels bowed down before Him when He was in His preincarnate state, and they said He was "holy, holy, holy" (see Isaiah 6:3). He was in charge of the universe. He was fully equal to the Father and the Holy Spirit. Jesus wasn't kicked out of heaven because of something He'd done; He voluntarily left heaven to go on a rescue mission. He came to this little lost planet to save us—a race of beings created in His image.

David said we were all born in sin and shaped in iniquity (see Psalm 51:5). But Jesus—though born in sin—never sinned in thought, word, or deed. All His actions are and always have been beyond reproach.

It is a spiritual reality that was the fulfillment of the prophecy of Genesis 3:15.

The wounded Champion

As a Champion battling for His people, Jesus was "wounded for our transgressions, he was bruised for our iniquities: the chastisement of our peace was upon him; and with his stripes we are healed" (Isaiah 53:5).

Jesus did have many wounds. He was wounded spiritually: He received a heavy blow in the Garden of Gethsemane. As He felt the weight of our sins descending upon Him, He felt their enormity; and His spirit, His very psyche, was wounded. "Then cometh Jesus with them unto a place called Gethsemane, and saith unto the disciples, Sit ye here, while I go and pray yonder. And he took with him Peter and the two sons of Zebedee,

and began to be sorrowful and very heavy. Then saith he unto
them, My soul is exceeding sorrowful, even unto death: tarry
ye here, and watch with me" (Matthew 26:36–38).

Like all the other writers of Scripture, Matthew chose
with great care the words with which he recorded his account. The Greek word that was translated "sorrowful and
very heavy" in the King James Version of Matthew's account
is *ad monein*. The primary meaning of this word is "to be sore
dismayed." This word seems to have been used of the dismay
that an unexpected calamity produces. Mark said that Jesus
was "sore amazed."

It seems that Jesus suddenly saw in full detail—in "digitized
Technicolor," if you please—what was about to happen to Him,
and the prospect overwhelmed Him. The burden was crushing.

Suddenly, and yet perhaps slowly, Jesus began to feel the
mental agony that developed as for the very first time He was
cut off from the Father—to say nothing of the confirmation that
the people who hated Him and wanted to destroy Him were
about to accomplish their nefarious, evil, despicable intention.

On top of this, there was the agony both of knowing that
He was innocent and didn't deserve the torment and of knowing that it was one of His "friends"—more than that—that it
was a person who had been a disciple of His who would betray Him. Imagine facing a situation knowing that a man you
had taught and had given a position of great responsibility in
your firm—someone whose feet you had washed and who
had spent three and a half years with you—was now going
to deliver you to people who would kill you! That the one to
whom you had entrusted the funds of your business was now

betraying you with a kiss. "Yea, mine own familiar friend, in whom I trusted, which did eat of my bread, hath lifted up his heel against me" (Psalm 41:9).

How low!

Jesus experienced extreme mental agony—"the dark night of the soul"—when He knew that no one was coming to His rescue. He felt all alone.

Yes, He realized that in His preincarnation state He and the Father and the Spirit had agreed on this rescue mission, but what was open to Him before He became a man was now closed to Him. Scripture doesn't suggest that He ever used His divine nature to ease His way through the passion. In fact, He also had to suffer the fear of not knowing whether His sacrifice would satisfy the claims of God's holy law. He didn't know whether He would come out of the grave and embrace life again.

Imagine that! Imagine being the Healer of humanity, the Creator of the universe, the Giver of life, and not knowing whether you would return to life after you made the ultimate sacrifice!

Yes, Jesus suffered torment of the soul. He was wounded emotionally, spiritually, and mentally as well as physically. The men closest to Him abandoned Him and ran, trying to save themselves.

And of course He was wounded physically. He was beaten, and then He was scourged two times, and that with a whip even more damaging than a cat-o'-nine-tails. The first scourging ripped His back open, enabling the second one to tear even deeper into it. Then He was nailed to a cross, where He hung naked for both friends and enemies to see. And all of this when He was completely innocent, the person prefigured and portrayed in the Garden of Eden by the innocent animal that was slain to provide clothing for Adam and Eve.

Jesus was battered, bloodied, bruised, executed, and left for dead. But He wasn't defeated. Though He was down, He wasn't out.

When Jesus was on the cross, Satan thought he had scored a knockout and won the fight. But though he had knocked Jesus down and it looked as though He'd been knocked out, He hadn't been. He was just staying "down for the count."

The "count" lasted three days, and when it ended, Jesus got to His feet again. Praise God, on the third day Jesus rose!

In our battles with sin and Satan, there are times when we may appear to be beaten. But we don't have to accept defeat. We may have been knocked down, but we can win the match.

How can we win? In chapter 7, I'll point out four practices that increase a person's spiritual strength. But beginning with the right basis has a lot to do with whether we stay in the fight. Our expectations may determine whether or not we are successful. I'll close this chapter by listing four crucial ones.

- *We must prepare for the battle.* All champions prepare for the battles that will test them. We must prepare by worshiping God, praying, and reading the Bible. Doing this will fix our minds on Jesus and teach us to trust Him.
- *We must remember that God hasn't left us to face the foe all by ourselves.* David wasn't alone when he fought Goliath. The God he had praised when he was back home tending sheep was with him.
- *We must believe that with God on our side, we can't lose.*

Through Isaiah, God told the people of Israel that if they followed His guidance, "no weapon that is formed against thee shall prosper" (Isaiah 54:17). John quoted Jesus as saying, "Whatsoever is born of God overcometh the world" (1 John 5:4). And Paul wrote, "We are more than conquerors through him that loved us" (Romans 8:37). These promises are meant for us.

· *Following the example of Jesus, our Champion, we must never give in, never give up, never quit.*

Diana Nyad was eight years old when she first dreamed of swimming the 110 nautical miles from Havana, Cuba, to Key West, Florida. She first attempted to make the swim in 1978, and she tried two more times in 2011 and once again in 2012, but she failed all four times.

However, Diana never lost her dream or her belief that she could fulfill it. At an age when most people have stopped looking for challenges, when they've given up on quests they've ignored since childhood, when they're dreaming about sitting back to enjoy the "golden years," she kept working at meeting the challenge.

And she succeeded! In 2013, when she was sixty-four years old, she finally made that historic swim.

In the battle we're in, we should never, ever give up. We're never too old to achieve the goals God has given us. And though living like Jesus may appear to be something each person must ultimately do alone, we have the support of the Holy Spirit, of the angels, and of those of our friends who are truly spiritual.

Jesus, the ultimate Champion, won the battle against sin and Satan, and He'll enable us to win that battle too. Let's rejoice in His victory, knowing that it means that in Him, we'll be winners too!

Endnote

1.   Ellen G. White, *Steps to Christ* (Mountain View, CA: Pacific Press®, 1956), 43.

Chapter 7

Jesus, Our Model

All great leaders model what they want people to believe and to do, and Jesus, the greatest leader of all time, certainly modeled what He taught. As His disciples, we believe that He is the Son of God, the Savior of the world—and our Example. In fact, He is our *supreme* Example; the model human being; the One whom we try to emulate.

In the previous chapter we saw Jesus as our Champion. He has won the battle against sin and Satan for us. He's the Savior, the one who has provided salvation for us. That's a good thing, because we can't save ourselves.

However, that doesn't mean that in the spiritual realm we have nothing to do. Though Jesus has conquered sin and the devil for us, we have a role to play in removing them from our lives and in becoming more like Jesus—in developing a character like His.

Jesus used four spiritual practices to strengthen His connection with God and thus to have the spiritual strength to defeat our evil opponent. In this He was our model, our example. The more we use these practices, the stronger our connection with God will be, the more battles we will win, and the more like Jesus we will become.

In this chapter you will find what those spiritual practices are and how to use them.

Do what pleases God

First, Jesus models for us a godly goal: that of pleasing the Father. Jesus Himself said it directly: "I always do what pleases him" (John 8:29, NIV).

Jesus loved to do His Father's will, and His Father and our Father are one and the same. That suggests that the Father appreciates our willingness to, like Jesus, "do what pleases him."

We can please the Father as Jesus did when we love Him. When we truly love Him, we'll surrender self and selfishness and do what He has asked us to do.

Think about it: love motivates us to try to please the one we love. This is true not only of romantic love but also of the love that we feel for God. It is what motivates us to become followers, disciples, of Jesus. This love isn't primarily a feeling; it's a choice, a decision, an act of the will that moves us to surrender and submit.

Obedience is hard only when our selfish wills are in the ascendency. Jesus lived a life of surrender and submission, and that made it easier for Him to obey. We too will find it easier to obey when we love God and are surrendering daily to Him.

To His disciples—us today as well as those of the first century of this era—Jesus said, "If you love Me, keep My commandments" (John 14:15, NKJV). We often read this text as a command, and it is. But it's also a statement of fact: if we do love Jesus, we will do what He speaks of, whether it's in the form of a request or of a command.

God Himself spoke the Ten Commandments, and then He wrote them in stone and gave them to Moses, His messenger, to give to those who claimed to be His people. (See Deuteronomy 5.) But God didn't give those commandments to the Israelites alone. He gave them to them to share with the world.

Often the Ten Commandments are called "the law of Moses," which suggests that Moses originated the Ten Commandments. However, we should remember that God was the first to give those commandments to anyone. Moses' role was merely to take what God had given him and to pass it along to Israel. Moses told us only what God told him to tell us.

Of course, when God gave His law to the Israelites, they misused it. When Jesus came to earth, He tried to correct their mistake. He summarized what message God meant the law to convey to people when He told His questioning audience that every word the prophets wrote was focused on bringing people to love God and to love people (Matthew 22:37–40). Here's how Matthew put it in his Gospel: "Hearing that Jesus had silenced the Sadducees, the Pharisees got together. One of them, an expert in the law, tested him with this question: 'Teacher, which is the greatest commandment in the Law?'

"Jesus replied: ' "Love the Lord your God with all your heart and with all your soul and with all your mind." This is the first and greatest commandment. And the second is like it: "Love your neighbor as yourself." All the Law and the

Prophets hang on these two commandments' " (Matthew
22:34–40, NIV).

Jesus chose to love the Father. He taught that loving God
was the first and greatest commandment.

Grace doesn't hide sin or whitewash it. Rather, it releases
the power of God in us. As we humble ourselves before God,
divine grace teaches us to how to obey God and brings us into
harmony with His will for us.

Grace is what I call one of God's indispensables when it
comes to salvation. "Christ says, 'Without Me ye can do nothing' [John 15:5]. Divine grace is the great element of saving
power; without it all human efforts are unavailing."[1] We need
Jesus and all His merits to please God and to live with Him
one day in eternal glory.

These admonitions remind us that God has provided
everything, yes, everything we need to live a victorious life in
this world. What a glorious thought! We actually have power
from God to win the battle as Jesus did.

Talk with God

When we love someone, we talk with that person regu-
larly. So, by His example, Jesus shows us another requirement
for powerful living—prayer.

"In the morning, rising up a great while before day, he
went out, and departed into a solitary place, and there prayed"
(Mark 1:35). "And it came to pass in those days, that he went
out into a mountain to pray, and continued all night in prayer
to God" (Luke 6:12).

This is a key to Jesus' victory: He submitted to the Father in prayer. Sometimes He arose early in the morning, long before sunrise, and prayed to God through hours of uninterrupted solitude. Not knowing what the day might bring, He "checked in" with the Holy Spirit to receive His orders. He submitted Himself to the will of God daily. Hourly. Moment by moment.

Sometimes He spent the entire night in prayer: "It was in hours of *solitary prayer* that Jesus in His earthly life received wisdom and power. Let the youth follow His example in finding at dawn and twilight a quiet season for communion with their Father in heaven. And throughout the day let them lift up their hearts to God. At every step of our way He says, 'I the Lord thy God will hold thy right hand, . . . Fear not; I will help thee.' Isaiah 41:13."[2]

Not surprisingly, prayer was one of the practices that Jesus focused on. He constantly and consistently communed with God, and His practice matched what He taught. There was no deviation between what He taught and what He lived. Let's look some more at what He taught about prayer:

> When thou prayest, thou shalt not be as the hypocrites are: for they love to pray standing in the synagogues and in the corners of the streets, that they may be seen of men. Verily I say unto you, they have their reward. But thou, when thou prayest, enter into thy closet, and when thou hast shut thy door, pray to thy Father which is in secret; and thy Father which seeth in secret shall reward thee openly. But when ye pray,

use not vain repetitions, as the heathen do: for they think that they shall be heard for their much speaking. Be not ye therefore like unto them: for your Father knoweth what things ye have need of, before ye ask him. After this manner therefore pray ye: Our Father which art in heaven, Hallowed be thy name. Thy kingdom come, Thy will be done in earth, as it is in heaven. Give us this day our daily bread. And forgive us our debts, as we forgive our debtors. And lead us not into temptation, but deliver us from evil: For thine is the kingdom, and the power, and the glory, for ever. Amen. For if ye forgive men their trespasses, your heavenly Father will also forgive you: But if ye forgive not men their trespasses, neither will your Father forgive your trespasses (Matthew 6:5–15).

Note the simplicity and directness of Jesus' model prayer. No high-sounding words, no deep theological jargon, no repetitiveness, no phrases to mindlessly repeat. Jesus simply talked to God. He acknowledged God as our eternal holy Father; asked that His heavenly reign be extended to earth, and asked for the basic needs of humanity: food, deliverance from evil, and forgiveness as we forgive those who have sinned against us.

Paul gave a very definitive listing of the armor of God in Ephesians 6:10–17. He said it includes truth, righteousness, the gospel, faith, salvation, and the Word of God. And then He says that all the armor should be "put on" in prayer: "Praying always with all prayer and supplication in the Spirit, and watching thereunto with all perseverance and supplication for all saints" (verse 18).

"Our only sure defense against besetting sins is prayer, daily and hourly prayer. . . . Prayer is necessary, and we should not wait for feeling, but pray, earnestly pray, whether we feel like it or not. Heaven is open to our prayers. Prayer is the channel that conducts our gratitude and yearnings of soul for the divine blessing to the throne of God, to be returned to us in refreshing showers of divine grace."[3]

Without prayer, we won't receive all that God wants to give us, and we're likely to have the delusion that we're OK just as we are. Submissive, confessing prayer brings us into the throne room of God, where we see ourselves as we really are and realize our need of the grace we can obtain only from Him.

Oh, to be like Daniel, who felt his need of God so deeply that he wouldn't budge from the routine of his prayer life even when threatened with death. Daniel's view of this discipline molded his life and service. It played an important role in helping him to continue to be a disciple of God. It seems to me that Daniel had found a source of power in his experience of prayer. He had found the source of the power that enabled him to live a God-centered life.

Consider this commentary: "In order to have spiritual life and energy, we must have actual intercourse* with our heavenly Father. Our minds may be drawn out toward Him; we may meditate upon His works, His mercies, His blessings; but this is not, in the fullest sense, communing with Him. In order

---

* As used here, the word *intercourse* doesn't refer to sexual relations. It means intimate communication—opening ourselves to God, telling Him all about ourselves: our burdens and our blessings, our fears and our desires.

to commune with God, we must have something to say to Him concerning our actual life."[4]

Jesus prayed about His actual life. He prayed passionately— pouring out His soul in His prayer. That's where He got the strength to fight the toughest battle anyone has ever faced, and to be victorious.

Memorize God's Word

Third, Jesus memorized the powerful, power-filled words of Scripture, so when the evil one came at Him full force, He had an armory of godly power with which to resist him. He found power in the Word of God.

> The tempter came to him and said, "If you are the Son of God, tell these stones to become bread."
>
> Jesus answered, "It is written: 'Man does not live on bread alone, but on every word that comes from the mouth of God.'"
>
> Then the devil took him to the holy city and had him stand on the highest point of the temple. "If you are the Son of God," he said, "throw yourself down. For it is written:
>
> 'He will command his angels concerning you, and they will lift you up in their hands,
>
> so that you will not strike your foot against a stone.'"
>
> Jesus answered him, "It is also written: 'Do not put the Lord your God to the test.'"

Again, the devil took him to a very high mountain and showed him all the kingdoms of the world and their splendor. "All this I will give you," he said, "if you will bow down and worship me."

Jesus said to him, "Away from me, Satan! For it is written: 'Worship the Lord your God, and serve him only.' "

Then the devil left him, and angels came and attended him (Matthew 4:3–11, NIV).

Obviously, Jesus spent time memorizing Scripture, which at that time meant the Old Testament. Thus He was able to meet the tempter with the power of the written Word of God. "It is written . . ." was His response to the temptations the evil one brought to Him (see Matthew 4). Here we see lived out in real life the effectiveness of the psalmist's battle plan: "Thy word have I hid in mine heart, that I might not sin against thee" (Psalm 119:11).

Have we forgotten this vital source of power, carelessly neglecting to store up in our memory vault words from the Word? Jesus, and Daniel before Him, didn't. They knew that there was power in the Word. There still is. We can still find in the Word of God the power we need to overcome the evil one.

Early in my ministry, some members of a church of which I was the pastor hurt me deeply—so deeply that I felt the pain for years. One beautiful summer night when the moon was so large and bright that it lit up the entire sky, we had a midweek prayer meeting in which those who were present felt the presence and power of the Holy Spirit in a special way.

We pled with God to give us victory over our sins, to heal the sick among us, and to help us be instruments through which He could bring people to Himself.

That night the testimonies and the prayers were powerful. Unity pervaded the church sanctuary that night, and when we left for our homes, our hearts glowed because of what God had done for us. It was awesome.

But while I was driving home, a spirit of evil seemed suddenly to press into my mind. I thought about the church members who had treated me unkindly, and anger and resentment welled up within me. I wanted to get even.

As those feelings grew, I remembered something that had happened while I was still in school. When I came out of the house where I was living at the time, I found that a tire on my car was flat. And then I had noticed that all the cars on that street had at least one flat tire. Someone had purposely punctured all those tires.

When I thought of that incident, the thought arose—it was almost a suggestion—that I could get my revenge on those nasty church members that very night. I could buy an icepick at a hardware store and then drive to the homes of those nasty members, puncture their tires, and drive away. *I could get away with it!* I thought. *They'd never know that I had done it.*

It seems amazing that these thoughts came to me right after I had felt so strongly God's power and love and the sweetness of corporate worship. Then it seemed to me that I heard someone say, "Ricardo, that is not My way. I will take care of them in My own way in My own time," and I remembered that God tells His people not to seek revenge but to leave vengeance in His hands (see Deuteronomy 32:35).

I asked the Lord to forgive me for enjoying that selfish, sinful thought of doing evil to members of His family. I repented for harboring the thought the devil had suggested to me. Then Romans 6:14 came to my mind, and I repeated the first part of it: "Sin shall not have dominion over you: for ye are not under the law, but under grace." I repeated it silently, and then I spoke it out loud.

That's right, I spoke the powerful Word to myself, and instantly my thoughts changed as the Word of God gave me power to reject the temptation to get revenge. I prayed earnestly—with my eyes wide open as I drove—asking God to deliver me from that evil thought, and He did. I never again was tempted to seek revenge against those people—or anyone else.

Yes, Jesus modeled for us a spiritual life based on prayer and memorization of Scripture. But we must remember that prayer and Bible memorization are not ends in themselves. They're tools through which God can bring us into fuller fellowship with Himself. It is through being in touch with Jesus that we are changed into likenesses of Him. Only He can make us resemble Him in character—which is what I long to be.

I believe that Jesus struggled with temptation, though not just the way we do because His nature isn't exactly like ours. I believe that He had fallen flesh, yet He never yielded to sin. The fallen flesh in which He had lived while here on earth made Him a target of temptation. But He was able to resist the devil and all the evil suggestions that came to Him because He submitted to the Father through prayer and Scripture study.

Don't misunderstand me. I'm not suggesting that if we pray long enough and hard enough and correctly enough we'll automatically be saved. Nor am I saying that if we memorize enough of the right Bible passages we'll earn our way into heaven. Absolutely not. That would be a salvation by means of works, and the Bible is clear that we are not saved by our works: "It is by grace you have been saved, through faith—and this not from yourselves, it is the gift of God—not by works, so that no one can boast. For we are God's workmanship, created in Christ Jesus to do good works, which God prepared in advance for us to do" (Ephesians 2:8–10, NIV). What I am saying is that Jesus, our Model, has made clear what weapons we should use in our spiritual warfare.

I remember being in a barbershop one day when the conversation turned to me and I was asked, "What do you do?" When I answered that I was a pastor, a fellow there who appeared to be on the verge of inebriation began quoting verses from the Bible—and he was quoting them correctly. This fellow, even in his near-drunken state, was rattling off one text after another correctly!

I don't think the Bible spouter got the full impact of the force and purpose of Scripture memorization. As the psalmist said, "Thy word have I hid in my heart, *that I might not sin against thee*" (Psalm 119:11; emphasis added).

I'm not judging that guy. In fact, I pray that he's been able to overcome his drinking habit. I'm telling this story to illustrate that a mere repetition of Scripture, as if it were some kind of occult mantra, won't bring the spiritual victories that God meant to be the ground, the foundation of our relationship with Him. When, through His Word, we come to know Him, we will love Him and trust Him—and we will despise the things that disparage Him or oppose Him. Then the temptations that formerly overwhelmed us will lose their appeal, and we'll have the victory that we desire.

Serve needy people

A fourth arrow in Jesus' quiver of holy living is found in His ministry—in serving people in every way possible. The woman at the well, Nicodemus, Jairus's daughter, the woman who touched the hem of His garment, the paralytic at the pool of Bethesda—all these people benefited by Jesus' ministry. His healing of spiritual as well as physical illnesses was the overflow produced by the inward focus of the commitment to obey God, to pray, and to memorize Scripture.

Jesus reached out to help people. It's extremely important that we do the same thing now. Jesus didn't live in a prayer closet. His ministry—His life of service—extended beyond His praying and His study of Scripture, and it carried Him into the public square—the community. Yes, He went to church, but He also carried the church to people. As God incarnate, He *was* the church to all who let Him into their lives, into their selves.

But Jesus modeled even more. He also modeled compassion. Compassion is "an aspect of God's nature which is reflected in his sympathetic understanding of human weakness and his restoration of those in trouble."[5] In the Bible, compassion is a divine as well as a human quality. In the Revised

Standard Version, the word *compassion* is often used to translate the Hebrew *hāmal* and *rachmim,* which the Authorized Version has more frequently rendered by "to pity" and "to spare," and "mercy" and "tender mercies" respectively. Thus "compassion," "pity," and "mercy" can be regarded as synonyms.

In the New Testament, the original words are *eleeō* and cognate forms. These Greek words are translated by "have compassion," "have mercy," and "have pity." The other Greek words with similar meanings are *eleos,* which is always translated "mercy"; *oiktirō,* "have compassion"; and *oiktirmōn,* "merciful" and "of tender mercy."[6]

Compassion, mercy, and pity are all demonstrated in Jesus' life. He had compassion on suffering humanity. In fact, one can say that His rescue mission, His coming to earth from heaven, was driven by His compassion for His creation, which was separated from Him in the Garden of Eden by Adam and Eve's deception and self-centered choice. Nonetheless, God's compassion borne of love compelled Him to enact the plan of salvation that had been conceived prior to Creation. As someone has said, "Before there was sin, there was a Savior." I believe that this is true, because Jesus consistently demonstrated His compassion toward people who obviously needed it.

The compassion Christ manifested as He looked upon the multitude was not a strange thing to Him, for this love and compassion dwells in the heart of the Father. "God so loved the world, that He gave His only-begotten Son, that whosoever believeth in Him should not perish, but have everlasting life" [John 3:16]. It was compassion that brought Christ from heaven. It was compassion that led Him to clothe His divinity with humanity, that He might touch humanity. This led Him to manifest unparalleled tenderness and sympathy for man in his fallen condition.[7]

One source notes that Jesus had compassion on the crowds (see Matthew 9:36; 14:14; 15:32; Mark 6:34; 8:2). He was filled with compassion for the leper (Mark 1:41). He had compassion on the widow of Nain (Luke 7:13). Moved with compassion, He touched the blind men (Matthew 20:34). And His compassion makes Him a merciful and faithful high priest (Hebrews 2:17).[8]

Not only did Jesus have compassion during His life and ministry on earth, but He continues to relate to the children of God with compassion.

"But when he saw the multitudes, he was moved with compassion because they fainted and were scattered abroad, as sheep having no shepherd. Then saith he unto his disciples, the harvest truly is plenteous, but the laborers are few; pray ye therefore the Lord of the harvest, that he will send forth laborers into his harvest." Our work is plainly laid down in the word of God. Christian is to be united to Christian, church to church, the human instrumentality co-operating with the divine, every agency to be subordinate to the Holy Spirit, and all to be combined in giving to the world the good tidings of the grace of God.[9]

Jesus used parables as teaching devices through which He expertly connected the natural to the spiritual—thus enabling us to understand the spiritual. As I have heard my pastor say, "What's true in the natural [world] is true in the spiritual [world]." Jesus made that clear when He said that when we minister to the hungry, thirsty, homeless, naked, sick, and imprisoned, we are demonstrating the ministry of compassion toward Him (see Matthew 25).

How do we learn and emulate this aspect of Christianity? How do we become more compassionate?

Look to Jesus, Paul tells us. Study Him, and then, to the best of our abilities, we must do what He did.

I'm not an expert in Christianity, but I know that as we study the model Jesus presented to us and then seek to copy it, we change. Nike's slogan is "Just Do It." That's how we learn best. Just doing what Jesus did will have a powerful effect on us. It will awaken compassion within us.

But before we just do it, we should seek the anointing of the Spirit. Jesus pointed out that even He was dependent upon the Spirit of the Lord directing His ministry (see Luke 4:18, 19).

Jesus had a love for God that led Him to submit to Him by obeying Him. It also led Him to commune with God through prayer, to memorize the Word of God, and to live a life of compassion. As the Spirit works within us, we can live a life that resembles the life of Jesus.

Endnotes

1. Ellen G. White, *Testimonies for the Church* (Mountain View, CA: Pacific Press®, 1952), 5:583.
2. Ellen G. White, *Education* (Mountain View, CA: Pacific Press®, 1952), 259; emphasis added.
3. Ellen G. White, *Our Father Cares* (Hagerstown, MD: Review and Herald®, 1991), 244.
4. Ellen G. White, *Prayer* (Nampa, ID: Pacific Press®, 2002), 280.
5. M. H. Manser, *Dictionary of Bible Themes: The Accessible and Comprehensive Tool for Topical Studies* (London: Martin Manser, 2009).
6. J. W. Meiklejohn, "Compassion," in *New Bible Dictionary*, eds. D. R. W. Wood, I. H. Marshall, A. R. Millard, J. I. Packer, and D. J. Wiseman (Leicester, England, and Downers Grove, IL: InterVarsity Press, 1996).
7. Ellen G. White, "Our Work," *Signs of the Times*, August 25, 1898, par. 12.
8. C. A. Day, *Collins Thesaurus of the Bible* (Bellingham, WA: Logos Bible Software, 2009).
9. White, *General Conference Daily Bulletin*, February 28, 1893, 421, par. 19.

Chapter 8

Jesus, the Forgiving One

F ather, forgive them; for they know not what they do" (Luke 23:34).

Despite the mockery of the trial, despite the perjury of the witnesses, despite the arrogance of the accusers, despite being nearly overwhelmed by pain, Jesus prayed for those who were murdering Him *while they were in the act*!

What impelled Jesus to pray that God would forgive the people who were murdering Him?

Love.

Jesus prayed for those people because He loved them. He loved them because He was the Son of God. He loved them because He Himself was God.

Isn't that just like God? He loves people even when they're killing Him. He loves us even though we betray Him. Even though we compromise and cheat and lie and steal and lust and gossip and on and on. He loves us despite who we are and despite what we are—sinners by nature and sometimes by choice. God persistently loves us no matter what. In fact, none of the heavenly beings—the Father, Jesus, the Holy Spirit, the angels—will abandon us.

I read a story in a local newspaper about a woman whom

I know. I met her—Cynthia—while I served on the Co-
ordinated Committee for a Drug Free County in San Joaquin
County, California.

Cynthia's son is addicted to heroin. Cynthia has done
everything that she can for him. She has argued with him.
She has fought with him. She has prayed for him. She has locked
him out of the house. She has paid for him to go through a drug
treatment program. She has done everything but give up on
him. He's her son. She's his mother. She can't forsake her son.

What about God? Can He forsake us? Can He cast off
His people?

- "When my father and my mother forsake me, then
  the LORD will take me up" (Psalm 27:10).
- "Can a woman forget her sucking child, that she should
  not have compassion on the son of her womb? yea, they
  may forget, yet will I not forget thee" (Isaiah 49:15).

Humans may forget their own children, but God will
never, never, never forsake those who look to Him for help,
for forgiveness, for salvation. That's why Jesus prayed to His
Father, asking Him to forgive those who were crucifying Him.

Who was it that was crucifying Jesus?

The religious leaders of the Jewish people: the priests, the
Levites, the scribes. People who wanted other people to think
that they were holy.

And Roman soldiers: men who were "just doing their job."

And also the ignorant masses: people who had "inno-
cently" gotten caught up in the flow of things.

It was for these people—and for murderers, and thieves, and gossips, and adulterers, and hotheads; in other words, for all of us—that Jesus prayed.

> His mind passed from His own suffering to the sin of His persecutors, and the terrible retribution that would be theirs. No curses were called down upon the soldiers who were handling Him so roughly. No vengeance was invoked upon the priests and rulers, who were gloating over the accomplishment of their purpose. Christ pitied them in their ignorance and guilt. He breathed only a plea for their forgiveness,—"for they know not what they do."[1]

"In a broader sense, this prayer includes all sinners to the end of time, for all are guilty of the blood of Christ."[2]

What was Jesus doing when He prayed for His Father to forgive His murderers? In essence, He was praying that His Father and His murderers be reconciled. Jesus wanted to save everyone, even those who were nailing Him to the cross!

I find it amazing that Jesus was willing to pray for the forgiveness of those who took His life. I find it amazing that the Father would even consider forgiving those who crucified His Son. I also find it amazing that God is willing to forgive me of my sins.

The reality of the matter is that God is willing to forgive me—and anyone else and everyone else who will repent and confess their sins in the name of Jesus.

The fact that Jesus prayed for His tormentors was not enough in and of itself to save them from the condemnation they deserved. Although salvation was offered to them, that offer was conditioned upon their acceptance of Jesus as Lord and Savior.

That's true now too. If we desire to be saved, if Christ's prayer for our forgiveness is to benefit us, then we must accept Jesus as Lord and Savior—as our Master.

Following Jesus' example

To be saved, we must submit ourselves to Him and live as His disciples, implementing the teachings that He has given us and emulating His righteous example. We must live as Jesus did, ready to forgive as He forgave.

Jesus can teach us to forgive because He knows how to forgive—and what forgiveness costs. He can require us to forgive because He is Lord and Master of a kingdom where love reigns in the hearts of its citizens.

He can demand that we forgive because He wants the best for us, and He knows that it is only those who live where people hold no grudges, harbor no hate, and foster no animosity who can experience true love, ultimate love.

Jesus even taught that we receive forgiveness only as we give it to others (see Matthew 6:12–14). Jesus' teaching would be mere rhetoric if it weren't for His actions; if it weren't for His example. His actions give validity to His words.

Murdered by the ignorant

Those who murdered Jesus were ignorant. That's a sophisticated way of saying "they didn't know nothing."

They didn't know whom they had laid their hands on. They didn't know whom they had whipped in Pilate's court-yard. They didn't know whose head they had pierced with a crown of thorns, or whose face they had slapped.

They didn't know the Man they were beating was the King of glory in humble expression. They didn't know that the Person they were striking was the One who had shaped the butterfly and taught it to fly.

They didn't know that the One upon whom they had forced a crown of thorns was the One who would give His people a crown of life. They didn't know that the One whom they were jeering would one day hear them weep and wail and gnash their teeth.

They didn't know that one day they would cry out, plead-ing for the rocks and mountains to "fall on us, and hide us from the face of him that sitteth on the throne" (Revelation 6:16).

They didn't know who Jesus was.

Oh yes, they had heard about Jesus, but they didn't know who He was!

The priests didn't know. The Roman soldiers didn't know. The mob didn't know.

You see, when our minds are filled with sinful thoughts, we don't know nothing.

Sin tempts us to love the things that will destroy us.

It makes us rationalize away our guilt.

It makes us think we're wearing godly clothes when we're actually naked.

It makes us think we're rich when in reality we're poor.

It makes us think that we're having a good time when the truth is that we're miserable.

It makes us think we are handsome or pretty when in reality we're covered with the warts of evil.

It blinds us so that we don't recognize the Son of God for who He is.

Do you know Jesus?

Do you know who He is?

He's the Lily of the valley.

He's the bright morning Star.

He's the fairest of ten thousand.

Everybody ought to know Him!

When we're sick, Jesus is our doctor.

When we're broke, He's our banker.

When we're hungry, He's our grocer.

When we're lonely, He's our friend.

When we're frightened, He's our security.

When we're weak, He's our strength.

Do you know Him?

If you don't, you need to become acquainted now! Jesus died on the cross so that your sins could be forgiven. He lives today to rescue you from the results of your wicked ways. He lives to help you and to ennoble you. Heaven rejoices whenever someone gets to know Jesus.

Time and time again we human beings have tried to save ourselves, but we have always failed. We'll continue to fail until we commit ourselves fully to God through Jesus Christ. We each need to pray, "Father, forgive me, for I don't know what I'm doing."

Jesus wants to give us the fullness of His love. If we will accept Him, we'll feel His presence, experience His power, and bask in the fullness of His love. He promises us prosperity, joy, and happiness while we live on earth, and eternal life with Him on the earth made new.

Endnotes

1. Ellen G. White, *The Desire of Ages* (Mountain View, CA: Pacific Press®, 1940), 744.
2. Francis D. Nichol, ed., *The Seventh-day Adventist Bible Commentary* (Washington, DC: Review and Herald®, 1980), 5:876.

Chapter 9

Jesus, the Faultless One

To say merely that Jesus was arrested so inadequately communicates what happened as to be almost a lie. It borders on the false and the ridiculous. Jesus was set up, fingered, ratted on. A stool pigeon turned Him in. And the one who delivered Him to those who wanted to eliminate Him was one of His own. One who had traveled with Him for three full years. One who had eaten with Him and had slept where He slept.

Jesus was betrayed by one to whom He had given the gift of healing and the power to cast out demons. He was betrayed by one whom He considered to be the brightest and best of the group. He was betrayed by the one who was entrusted with the group's moneybag.

Judas, who had pretended to be Jesus' disciple—His friend—betrayed Him.

"It was not an enemy that reproached me; then I could have borne it: neither was it he that hated me that did magnify himself against me; then I would have hid myself from him: but it was thou, a man mine equal, my guide, and mine acquaintance. We took sweet counsel together, and walked unto the house of God in company" (Psalm 55:12–14).*

Sometimes, people who we think are our friends are our worst enemies. Sometimes, people who support us when things are going well turn against us when adversity arises.

Judas. The name rings down through the ages with infamy. It brings feelings of revulsion and disrespect. No parents name their son *Judas.* Other names used at that time—*Matthew, Luke, John,* and *Thomas*—are still popular today; but not *Judas.* I've never heard even of a dog named *Judas.* That name has connotations of evil, of shame—all because the man who bore it betrayed the Lord and Savior Jesus Christ.

Matthew tells us when Judas determined to betray Jesus. Apparently, he left that last supper because Jesus had rebuked him and that bruised his ego. He was embarrassed. His feelings were hurt. After all, wasn't he the treasurer? Shouldn't he then have a say as to how most of the money was to be spent?

John 12:6 tells us that Judas was a thief. Imagine that: the church treasurer was a thief! Jesus knew what Judas had been doing. He didn't tell the other disciples because He was trying to save Judas, and exposing him would have raised a barrier between them.

Some of us can't stand being rebuked by anyone. We become angry and bent out of shape. Our egos recoil. And the truer the rebuke, the angrier we become! Is that because our conversion is only partial? Or perhaps we haven't taken even the first step yet.

In the case of Judas, the fact is that he had never been converted.

---

*   This is a Messianic psalm. Though David wrote it about his own experience, it speaks also, and perhaps primarily, of the Messiah to come.

Think of it! Judas had been walking and talking with Jesus for more than three years; he had kept Jesus at a distance all that time! Judas proves that it is possible to be involved with righteous matters and to associate with righteous people and still be corrupt.

How do I know that Judas was never converted? Jesus said as much: "Have not I chosen you twelve, and one of you is a devil?" (John 6:70). In other words, He was saying that one of the disciples was under the influence of the devil.

Jesus had said something similar to Peter (Mark 8:33), but there was a big difference between Peter and Judas. Jesus knew that Judas was insincere, and He knew that Peter was sincere. Though misguided and impetuous, Peter was dedicated to Jesus. Judas wasn't. He was dedicated to himself. He was dedicated to getting whatever he wanted by any means necessary.

All of us are dedicated either to God's program or to our own. And to make what benefits us our primary concern is really to be dedicated to Satan. However, as was true of His treatment of Judas, Jesus will keep us in His family as long as there is hope that we may come to trust ourselves to Him. There's no guarantee that we will be saved just by attending church services. We must surrender our hearts to God daily and die to self daily.

Judas could have let God have His way with him. The choice was his. He decided not to. We each must make that decision too. What will you choose?

The kiss

The way Judas betrayed our Lord was despicable. It was low down. It was bad enough that it was one of Jesus' disciples that betrayed Him, but it was even worse that this hypocritical, back-stabbing, two-faced, fallen disciple betrayed Him with a kiss!

Jesus noted the cruel irony of it. He asked Judas, "Betrayest thou the Son of man with a kiss?" (Luke 22:48). That was more an indictment than a question.

When we think of a kiss, we think of something positive. We think of husbands and wives expressing their love for each other. We think of parents kissing their children as they put them to bed at night. And Paul even told church members that they should express their love and concern for each other with a holy kiss (see 2 Corinthians 13:12).

However, kissing can also have negative connotations. Apparently, members of the Mafia sometimes give someone the "kiss of death," which is a kiss that tells those who receive it that they are marked for death. They are marked for ex-ecution. In the vernacular, they are marked to be hit, to be rubbed out.

Long before the Mafia existed, Judas gave Jesus the "kiss of death" to identify Him to the mob that came to arrest Him. What hypocrisy! What evil! Pretending to greet Jesus with affection, when his kiss was actually the means of turning his Lord over to the evil mob so that they could murder Him.

Judas soon realized what he had done. He soon admitted to himself and to those who wanted to be rid of Jesus that the Person he had betrayed was the innocent Lamb of God. Afraid of the consequences, Judas sought to undo the deed. But his "confession" came too late, and it came from the wrong mo-tivation. He still loved money, but he loved his own skin even more. His feeble attempt to save himself was only a further revelation of his self-centeredness.

How much did Judas get for his kiss?

Judas betrayed Jesus for thirty pieces of silver. That was the price of a common slave. This silver coin was the equivalent of the Persian shekel, which was equal to the Greek *statēr,* which was worth a few of our dollars. That isn't much. So, Judas sold the Savior of humankind for a couple hundred dollars or so.

The old saying "every man has his price" is still true of most people—maybe not with money and not as blatant a betrayal as was Judas's. But we're tempted to accept the evil one's promises of pleasure and fame and wealth in exchange for turning from the life God calls us to live. We would do well to ask ourselves what temptations pull us most strongly away from Jesus—and then to ask Him to help us value our relationship with Him more than we value what the devil offers us.

Pilate's investigation

Eventually, the religious leaders of the Jews took Jesus to Pontius Pilate, the governor whom the Roman caesar had sent to rule over Jerusalem and the surrounding area. Through most of the year, the governor or procurator lived in Caesarea. Often, however, he would move to Jerusalem during the great Jewish festivals, to be on hand to put down any insurrections the Jews might attempt to start. The Passover was one of those important Jewish festivals, so at that time Pilate was living in his palace in Jerusalem.

Since the Jews didn't have the authority to execute anyone,

those who wanted Jesus dead had to make their case to Pilate, hoping to persuade him to give them that permission. Pilate wasn't much impressed with the people who were calling for Jesus' execution. But his curiosity was aroused, and he asked what charges had been brought against Him. The leaders of the Jews told him that Jesus was a malefactor—a "doer of evil," a criminal.

When Pilate attempted to find the exact nature of Jesus' crimes, he found no substance behind the charges that had been brought against Him. There was no evidence that Jesus had done anything illegal. Those who wanted Him dead told Pilate that Jesus talked about the temple in Jerusalem being destroyed and that He was a blasphemer because He claimed to be the Son of God.

Pilate didn't think that either of these supposed crimes warranted the death penalty. So, the leaders of the Jews appealed to Pilate's pride and to his fears. They told him that Jesus had also claimed to be the king of the Jews, which made Him guilty of plotting insurrection and rebellion against Caesar. And they said that if Pilate allowed Jesus to live, he would be supporting someone who was rebelling against Rome and against Caesar's rule. So, Pilate was keeping this rebel alive at the risk of his career and likely of his own life. It was his job to see to it that things were kept under control.

Pilate talked privately with Jesus. He asked Him who He was. He asked Him about the truth. And then he tried to get rid of Jesus. He tried to persuade the Jews to take care of the matter (see John 18:31). He sent Jesus to Herod Antipas (Luke 23:7). He attempted to release Jesus as the pardoned Passover prisoner (John 18:39). He had Jesus scourged in the hope of arousing pity for Him and thus of saving Him from the death penalty (see Luke 23:22).

Like Pilate, some of us try to dismiss Jesus as not being relevant to our lives, our wants and needs. But Jesus won't allow anyone to dismiss Him. We have to decide whether to accept Him as our Savior and whether we'll let Him have control of our lives. Like Pilate, we may try to wash our hands of Him, but we can't dismiss Jesus that easily.

The verdict

Three times on that fateful Friday, Pilate told the mob, "I find no fault in him!" (See John 18:38; 19:4, 6.) In other words, Pilate found Jesus innocent of the charges trumped up against Him. If we were to conduct our own investigation of the charges against Jesus, what would we find?

Nicodemus would tell us, "I thought I knew all about spiritual matters, being a leader in Israel and all, but I learned from Him that I must be born again of water and of the Spirit or I can't enter the kingdom of heaven. *I find no fault in this Man!*"

The woman at the well would witness, "I had lived with six different men without marrying any of them. This itinerant Jewish preacher revealed that He knew all about my promiscuous ways, yet He told me that despite my guilt, He would give me what He called 'living water'—He would so satisfy me that I would never thirst again. *I find no fault in this Man!*"

The adulterous woman brought to test Jesus would say,

"He didn't condemn me. Instead, He told me to go and sin no more. *I find no fault in this Man!*"

The thief on the cross would confess, "I was guilty of sin and evil. I was deserving of death. But while I hung on the cross next to Him, I asked Him to remember me when He received His kingdom, and in the midst of His agony, He promised to save me. *I find no fault in this Man!*"

And what would the devil admit? "I tempted Him in all things, yet He is still without sin. He said, 'Get behind me, Satan,' and I had to do it. And one day, even I will bow the knee to Him and say, *'I find no fault in this Man!'*"

Jesus has taught us to love God with all our hearts, minds, and souls. He has taught us to love our enemies. He has taught us that our heavenly Father loves us much more than the best earthly father loves his children. He has taught us that God wants to forgive our every sin. How could we say anything but *"We find no fault in this man"*?

Jesus gave sight to blind Bartimaeus.

He called Lazarus out of the ice-cold grip of death.

He set the demoniacs free.

He taught Mary Magdalene how to "just say No!"

I find no fault in this Man!

Jesus fed the hungry, gave water to the thirsty, and clothed the naked with His robe of righteousness.

I find no fault in this Man!

You may be thinking, *What the Bible says is good, brother preacher, but what do you say about Jesus?*

I have never met Jesus.

I have never heard His voice.

He has never touched me.

Yet I see Him every day.

If I listen, He tells me how to direct my every step.

Jesus has touched my life and changed it altogether.

You see, I once was wrapped in sin, but Jesus took me in.

I was stuck in the foul mire of this world, but Jesus set me free.

He didn't ask me for money; He just wants to be my Friend. He just wants to be my Savior and Lord. *I find no fault in this Man!*

What about you? If you will get to know Him, you'll find no fault in Him either.

Jesus said, "All that the Father giveth me shall come to me; and him that cometh to me I will in no wise cast out" (John 6:37).

If you come to Him, He'll accept you. He won't force Himself upon you, but neither will He cast you out.

You can live with Him in His Father's mansion, and He'll be your Friend, your Helper, your Savior, and your Guide for eternity. Just tell Him you're interested—that you want a home like that, and more important, you want a Friend like that.

If you ask, He'll make sure that it happens.

Chapter 10

Jesus, the Risen One

The claim that Jesus rose bodily from the dead is either the cornerstone of Christianity or its fatal flaw. If Jesus didn't rise from the dead, Christianity is a myth and billions of people have been deceived. If, on the other hand, He was resurrected, we can believe all that the Bible claims that Jesus said and did, and we have the guarantee that our sins have been forgiven, and we also have the assurance that we will rise from the grave and live eternally.

What reason do we have for believing that Jesus was actually raised to life after He was executed? There are at least three. The first is the empty tomb.

The Roman soldiers who crucified Jesus were professional executioners. They had no doubt crucified many people, and they knew when the people they crucified were dead. Before they took Jesus down from the cross, they examined Him to determine whether He was actually dead—and then, just to make sure that He was, they thrust a spear into His heart. They didn't allow Joseph of Arimethea to take Jesus' remains away until they were certain that He was dead.

When the Roman soldiers were satisfied that Jesus was dead, they allowed Joseph to take His body and place it in a tomb that had been cut into solid rock. The stone "door" to the tomb was rolled in front of the entrance, and a contingent of Roman soldiers—as many as sixteen of these human fighting machines—was assigned to guard the tomb. These men were trained to protect the entrance to the tombs they were assigned to guard and were skilled enough to hold off an entire battalion. In addition, the authorities placed a seal on the stone. Anyone who broke into the tomb without having official permission to do so would have drawn the wrath of the Romans upon himself.

But despite all of these precautions, when the believers arrived on Sunday morning, they found the stone rolled away and the tomb empty except for the bloodstained clothes in which Jesus had been buried. Jesus' body wasn't there. The empty tomb is a powerful testimony to the truthfulness of the claim that Jesus rose from the dead.

That empty tomb has challenged critics down through the years. Who would have been able to get past the guards, break into the tomb, and remove Jesus' body? And why would they have done it?

Some skeptics have suggested that Jesus' disciples stole His body. But this seems far-fetched. To do so, that group of cowards, who were hiding behind locked doors for fear that they would be next, would have had to overpower a fully armed contingent of Roman soldiers, roll a two-ton boulder away from the tomb's entrance, dispose of Jesus' body, and then manufacture a myth about His resurrection—one that, despite their differences, they all held to even though doing so meant that nearly all of them died painful deaths. That doesn't seem plausible.

Other critics have supposed that the religious leaders who persuaded Pilate to OK the crucifixion disposed of His body when He died. But this suggestion has some serious flaws as well. Those religious leaders were doing all they could to undermine the faith of the people who had become followers of Jesus. If they had the body of Jesus, they could have proved He was a fraud not worth following simply by displaying it. That would demonstrate beyond challenge that He was dead and gone, killing the appeal of Christianity at its beginning. But the Jewish religious leaders couldn't make that argument because they didn't have His body.

In fact, no one else had Jesus' body either, because He was no longer dead. He had indeed been raised to life again.

Christianity rises or falls on the empty tomb. It is a silent, irrefutable witness that critics cannot explain away. The leaders of every other religion have stayed dead after they died. Their bones are decaying in the ground. But that's not true of Jesus. He claimed that He would rise from death on the third day, and that's exactly what He did.

If Jesus didn't rise from the dead, then where was His body?

The Romans no doubt wanted to have it, because not having it made their soldiers look either incompetent or corrupt.

The disciples didn't have it, and they wouldn't have wanted to have it because it would increase the dangers they faced as His associates, and it would be evidence that His teachings were false.

And the Jewish authorities didn't have it either. If they had it, they could have used it to quell the claims Jesus had made about being the Messiah who would establish the promised kingdom.

The empty tomb validates the claim that Jesus was resurrected.

The many witnesses

The second evidence for the truth of the claim that Jesus was resurrected is the number of people who saw Him after His death. These people believed because they saw Him with their own eyes. When they told others why they believed in Jesus, they could not only say, "His tomb is empty," but also, "We know He's alive because we saw Him!"

The Bible mentions some twelve times when Jesus' disciples saw Him. Altogether, more than five hundred people saw, in person, the living Christ. For instance, after His resurrection, Jesus spoke to a woman in the cemetery where He had been entombed. Later that same day, He appeared to frightened followers of His who were huddled in Jerusalem. It's not hard to imagine how much courage that brought them! And on the evening of that day, He walked with two of His followers as they headed home.

Acts 1:3 sums it up: "After his suffering, he showed himself to these men and gave many convincing proofs that he was alive. He appeared to them over a period of forty days and spoke about the kingdom of God" (NIV).

Jesus appeared to believers and doubters, to tough-minded

people and tenderhearted souls. Several people saw Him on more than one occasion. Some saw Him when they were alone, and some when they were in large groups. Some at night, and some during the day.

The apostle Paul laid it all out in a letter he wrote to people who had become Christians a decade or two after Jesus returned to heaven. He wrote, "What I received I passed on to you as of first importance: that Christ died for our sins according to the Scriptures, . . . and that he appeared to Peter, and then to the Twelve. After that, he appeared to more than five hundred of the brothers at the same time, most of whom are still living, though some have fallen asleep" (1 Corinthians 15:3–6, NIV).

More than five hundred could testify that they had seen the resurrected Christ. Christianity was launched in the place where Jesus lived and taught and healed. Many people who had seen Him then were still alive and able and willing to talk about it. In effect, the early church could say, "If you don't believe us, ask these people. They saw Him with their own eyes."

In what was apparently the first sermon the disciple Peter preached, he summarized what the prophets wrote about Jesus and how Jesus fulfilled their prophecies. Then he laid out the details surrounding Jesus' death, and he concluded his sermon by saying, "God has raised this Jesus to life, and we are all witnesses of the fact" (Acts 2:32, NIV). Peter preached this sermon in the heart of Jerusalem—the very city where Jesus had been crucified and buried. The people to whom he was preaching knew that the tomb was empty and that Jesus had appeared to hundreds of people.

One of the letters Peter wrote makes it clear that he wanted his readers to know that he didn't make up the claim that Jesus was resurrected. Peter saw the resurrected Jesus. He talked with Him. And he even attended a fish fry Jesus put together on the beach one day. So in his letter he wrote: "We did not follow cleverly devised tales when we made known to you the power and coming of the Lord Jesus Christ, but we were eyewitnesses of His majesty" (2 Peter 1:16, NASB).

The changed lives

There's one more compelling argument for the resurrection: changed lives. Those who met the resurrected Jesus were totally transformed—changed in ways only the divine Son of God had the power to effect. Jesus' resurrection is validated by the changed lives of His followers.

Something happened to radically reorient the original group of followers. When Jesus was put to death, the disciples were scared to death. They ran and hid. Jesus, their Leader, had been executed. They feared they would be next.

But something happened that changed them completely. The book of Acts pictures them openly preaching about Jesus in the temple—a very public place, and a place where those who brought about Jesus' death were sure to be. John 20:19, 20 portrays for us a scene that would forever change their outlook—and their lives: "Jesus came and stood among them and said, 'Peace be with you!' After he said this, he showed them his hands and side. The disciples were overjoyed when they saw the Lord" (NIV).

When Jesus entered the upper room, where the disciples were hiding from the men who had crucified Him, He didn't tell them He was deeply disappointed at their cowardice. He didn't rake them over the coals for running away from Him when He was arrested in the garden. He didn't tell them He found their cowardice deeply disappointing. Nor did He angrily ask why they didn't testify on His behalf at the trials held by the Sanhedrin and Pilate and Herod. Instead, He said, "Peace be with you."

Remember, Jesus was the Creator. At His word light overwhelmed darkness, and when He spoke, the sun and moon and stars, and solar systems, and galaxies, and life itself came into existence. So when He said, "Peace be with you," He wasn't merely telling the disciples that He wished them well. *He was creating peace and giving it to them.* This overwhelming divine peace cut through their guilt and their feelings of failure. It replaced their fear with joy. Peter, one of the three disciples who were closest to Jesus, was changed from a coward who had—three times—denied that he was a disciple of Jesus into a man of rock who became one of the pillars of the new church. The ordinary men and women who followed Jesus were transformed from frightened wimps into one of the most daring and effective missionary organizations the world has ever seen.

What motivated them to go everywhere and proclaim the message of the risen Christ? Did they do it for money? For power? For fame?

No. They all had been brought from doubt to determination, from confusion to conviction, from fear to faith. Notice how they died, and ask yourself whether people would die as these people did for what they knew was a fable:

- Matthew was killed for his faith in Ethiopia.
- Mark was dragged to death.
- Peter, Simeon, Andrew, and Philip were crucified.
- James was beheaded.
- Bartholomew was flayed alive.
- Thomas was pierced with lances.
- James the Less was thrown from the heights of the temple and then stoned.
- Jude was shot to death with arrows.
- And Paul was boiled in hot oil and beheaded.

All these men could have avoided death if they had been willing to say, "Jesus is dead." I believe the only thing that could possibly have turned these doubting, fearful men into bravely outspoken men who were so deeply committed to their gospel of the resurrected Jesus that they continued to preach it at the cost of their lives. Only people who were utterly convinced of the truth of their message would do that. The disciples refused to be silent because they knew Jesus was alive, and they believed that because He had eternal life, they would have it too!

We see the evidence that Jesus is alive and at work in the world not only in the changes in the life and character of believers who lived during the first century A.D. but also in the transformations wrought in those who have come to believe in the resurrected Christ all down through history and in our own era. The number of people whose lives have been changed through the power of the risen Christ runs into the billions, and it includes people of every race and tribe and nationality in the world. Despite the differences in their culture and life experiences, all these believers have been changed by the living Jesus Christ.

When the British signal corps tried to transmit the news of Wellington's victory over Napoleon at Waterloo, they managed to get only the first two words of the message across the Channel before fog descended and halted all further communication for three days. Those two words were "Wellington defeated—"

Those three days were days of desperate anxiety for the British, for they thought their hopes had been dashed in that battle. What rejoicing there was, then, when the fog lifted and they received the whole message: "Wellington defeated Napoleon at Waterloo"!

Jesus has changed my life. I can testify that His life-changing power is just as available to us today as it was to the group of frightened followers on resurrection day in the year A.D. 31.

Jesus was crucified nearly two thousand years ago. He hung on the cross for our sins. When He died, darkness descended on the earth, and heaven's angels heard the words "Jesus defeated—"

Death, like a deep, impenetrable fog, obscured humanity's hope in Christ. But when Jesus stepped out of the borrowed tomb three days later, the message that flashed throughout the universe was "Jesus defeated Satan at Calvary!"

"He lives, He lives, Christ Jesus lives today!
He walks with me and talks with me along life's
    narrow way.
He lives, He lives, salvation to impart!
You ask me how I know He lives?
He lives within my heart!"

Has Jesus changed your life? He will if you ask Him to. Tell
Him you want Him to live in your heart.

Chapter 11

Jesus, the Gracious One

am an avid consumer of news. I try to catch it daily on TV. I listen to it on the radio when I'm driving. I read it in newspapers and newsmagazines. And sometimes I check out the latest news stories via the Internet. While I don't consider myself a news junkie, I do like to stay informed—especially since current world events remind me of the nearness of Jesus' return.

Increasingly, I get the impression that there is nothing new or good about the news. It seems to be the same old story of nature's assaults on humanity and people's inhumanity to other people told over and over again, sometimes in nauseating detail—the only differences being the names, faces, and places and the escalating depravity.

We read of the greed of corporate managers who lay off the hourly workers while they vote themselves huge raises and bonuses. We hear of dictators who rob their countries of the wealth that could have been used to lift their impoverished citizens from the gutter of life. We hear allegations that some minister has fallen into a deep pit of immorality and vice, or that a politician has flip-flopped, disregarding the promises he or she made when campaigning.

None of this is surprising to students of the Bible. After all, Paul told Timothy that "in the last days perilous times shall come. . . . Evil men and seducers shall wax worse and worse, deceiving, and being deceived" (2 Timothy 3:1, 13).

We do know that in earth's last days the church and its members will face unprecedented peril. Paul listed a plethora of evils, and while I can't read his mind, it seems to me that he was alerting Timothy and the generations that followed to the encroachment of evil into the church itself.

How can we live in this increasingly evil world without being overcome by its wickedness? We must always keep in mind that we are not saved by anything we do. In fact, since we are sinners, the only "wage" we can earn is death. (See Romans 6:23.) That's why Paul tells us that it is by grace that we are saved through faith, and that grace "is the gift of God." We are not saved by our works, "lest any man should boast" (see Ephesians 2:8, 9).

The law isn't an apparatus we can use to save ourselves. It shows, it tells, it teaches, and it informs, but it doesn't perform. The law reveals the character of God, but it doesn't rescue us from sin. Grace doesn't diminish the law of God; rather, it functions as a copartner with the law in reaching and teaching us, thus preparing us to be overcomers in Christ so that we can have the full victory made possible by our loving, holy, heavenly Father.

Grace is granted to us when we put our faith, trust, and belief in God. It is more than the forgiveness that God freely gives us so that we are acceptable to Him in all His holiness. It is didactic in nature, teaching or tutoring us to yield to God. Grace empowers us, energizes us, enthuses us, and enables us to live for God. Paul told one of his protégés, "The grace of God that bringeth salvation hath appeared to all men, teaching us that, denying ungodliness and worldly lusts, we should live soberly, righteously, and godly, in this present world" (Titus 2:11, 12). And Ellen White commented, "It is not merely God's mercy and willingness to forgive; it is an active, energizing, transforming power to save."[1] The *Seventh-day Adventist Bible Commentary* notes, "Divine grace is the great element of saving power."[2] So, we recognize grace as being, among other things, power—power that God gives to us.

Our great High Priest

Paul tells us that since "we have a great high priest, that is passed into the heavens, Jesus the Son of God, let us hold fast our profession. For we have not an high priest which cannot be touched with the feeling of our infirmities; but was in all points tempted like as we are, yet without sin. Let us therefore come boldly unto the throne of grace, that we may obtain mercy, and find grace to help in time of need" (Hebrews 4:14–16).

Paul says here that we have a great High Priest. He is the only Mediator who represents us to God. (See 1 Timothy 2:5.) Because this great High Priest is in heaven mediating for us, we are to do two things. First, we are to hold fast our profession or confession. We who profess, we who confess Jesus as our Savior should not grow weak or weary. We should not let this cold world with its sinful standards freeze us out. We must look steadfastly to Jesus. When we do, He, the Son of righteousness, will warm our hearts.

And second, we are to come boldly to the throne of grace. We are not to approach God timidly or in fear of rejection. On the contrary, we are to come to Him confidently because He offers His grace freely to all who seek it.

The throne of grace is God's throne. It is called the throne of grace because the One who sits upon it is gracious. He is righteous, holy, pure, eternal, merciful, long-suffering, sanctified, omniscient, transcendent, and imminent. He is above and beyond sin, and He cannot be tempted. He is altogether lovely. He is not anxious for anyone to perish; in fact, He is seeking the lost so that they may be saved.

God isn't content to respond only to those who are already saved. God wants to save those who don't even know that they are lost. He sent His Son, incarnate, into this world so that we could know that He is love. At the throne of grace we obtain mercy. There we find forgiveness for sin, iniquity, and transgression. There we find the peace that passes all understanding. There we find the pardon of God.

Jesus can offer all of this to us because He died on the cross for us. He died so that we could be free from sin. He died so that we could be overcomers, filled with power. He died so that we could have eternal life.

Most of all, at the throne of grace we find help. I know I need help. I need all the help that I can get. I need the help of God every day of my life. I need His help to resist temptation. I need His help to be kind and loving. I need His help to endure suffering and hardship. I need His help to control my appetite and my temper. I need His help so that I won't become, on the one hand, a workaholic, or, on the other, indolent and lazy. I need the grace of God to help me love the unlovable. I need it to help me to love my enemies. I need God's grace because it alone can enable me to live the life of a Christian.

When we live under grace, a couple things happen. First, sin loses its attractiveness. We are born with a sinful, fallen nature. Paul wrote, "All have sinned, and come short of the glory of God; being justified freely by his grace through the redemption that is in Christ Jesus: whom God hath set forth to be a propitiation through faith in his blood, to declare his righteousness for the remission of sins that are past, through the forbearance of God; to declare, I say, at this time his righteousness: that he might be just, and the justifier of him which believeth in Jesus" (Romans 3:23–26).

When in faith we come to God through Jesus, we are forgiven and empowered. When, through the grace of God, we are justified, God regards us as if we had never sinned. And when we focus on what God the Father, God the Son, and God the Holy Spirit have done for us, we are no longer enamored with sin. It loses its appeal. It is no longer alluring. The spell, as it were, is broken.

When Jesus comes into our lives and we realize that it was our sins that cost Him His life on Calvary, then we don't want to have anything to do with sin. Then the things that we used to think were so thrilling, so much fun, we now consider hideous and hateful. When we are in Christ and He is in us, sin eventually becomes repulsive to us.

Second, we receive power to live the life of Christ. Through the person of the Holy Spirit, Jesus takes residence in our minds and hearts.

- "It is God which worketh in you both to will and to do of his good pleasure" (Philippians 2:13).
- "God would make known what is the riches of the glory of this mystery among the Gentiles; which is Christ in you, the hope of glory" (Colossians 1:27).
- "[May God] make you perfect in every good work to do his will, working in you that which is well pleasing in his sight, through Jesus Christ; to whom be glory for ever and ever. Amen" (Hebrews 13:21).

We especially need the grace of God in this final stage of earth's history. The apostle Peter tells us that we should "grow in grace, and in the knowledge of our Lord and Saviour Jesus Christ" (2 Peter 3:18).

Grow in grace

To grow in grace means to advance spiritually. If grace includes a dimension of power, and it does, then growing in grace means increasing our appropriation of spiritual power. God gives us this power to enable us to develop godly characters, and they, in turn, enable us to live godly lives. Growing Christians have as their goal developing characters that resemble the perfect character of the Lord and a mind that is able to think His thoughts after Him.

If Jesus is our Model, and I believe that He is, then we should see in Him the traits that He wants us to develop.

- Jesus helped and blessed others. We must do the same.
- Jesus' life was one of self-denial. We too must deny self.
- Jesus spent much time—sometimes all night— talking to His Father. We also need to bare our souls in prayer.
- Jesus attended the services of the temple even though He knew many of the religious leaders were corrupt and wicked. We also need to worship God with fellow believers.

We must grow in our knowledge of Jesus Christ. We do this by studying Him as He is revealed in the gospels of the New Testament. There we find His character and personality portrayed. There we see His kindness, love, obedience, humbleness, fearlessness, holiness, and willingness to forgive. There we discover Jesus' acts of power—we witness His complete victory over Satan as He conquers all diseases and vanquishes death. There we learn why He is called both the Lion of the tribe of Judah and the Lamb slain from the foundation of the earth. There we come to understand how, as our true High Priest, He represents us to God.

In order to receive this grace, we must meet the Grace Giver. We must meet Jesus.

We can meet Him in Gethsemane, where the sins of humanity weighed Him to the ground. Where, as the disciples slept, He pleaded with the Father, asking Him to find some other way than the cross to save us; but there was none.

We can meet Him at the cross of Calvary. He went there for us. He suffered and died so that we could live.

We can meet Him at the tomb borrowed from Joseph of Arimethea, where Jesus rested through the Sabbath, keeping it holy even in His death.

We can meet Him at the resurrection, as He exited from the tomb with the life that was His at Creation—life that was original, unborrowed, and underived.[3]

But we can meet Him in our daily walk too. We can meet Him where the distressed and weary live. He is there, for truly the Spirit of Christ longs to give them relief and bring them joy.

We can meet Him among the homeless. Jesus was homeless too. And the homeless ones need the compassion that Jesus can bring through us.

And most important, we can meet Him when we're on our knees. He is waiting for us there. Meeting Jesus, the Grace Giver, is truly the core of the gospel.

So, when we see the many evils humanity is suffering, we can remember Christ's desire to empower us through His grace so that we can carry on His work till He comes. Living in the grace of God will prepare us for whatever we may experience because it will keep us focused on God.

Do you know Jesus? Do you trust Him enough to give yourself to Him? To seek His forgiveness, and then to carry on His mission?

He's coming soon! That's the good news. Why not give yourself to Him today?

Endnotes

1.   F. D. Nichol, ed., *The Seventh-day Adventist Bible Commentary* (Washington, DC: Review and Herald®, 1980), 6:504.

2.   Ellen G. White, *Gospel Workers* (Washington, DC: Review and Herald®, 1948), 70.

3.   Ellen G. White, *The Desire of Ages* (Mountain View, CA: Pacific Press®, 1940), 530.

If you have been blessed by *Jesus Unlimited*, you might also like . . .

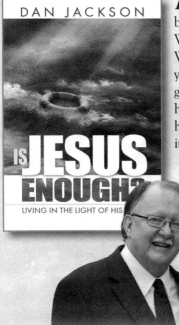

Is Jesus Enough?

by Dan Jackson

When is enough, enough? What will it take to satisfy your soul? In this age of self-gratification, how many cars, houses, bank accounts, motor homes, or swimming pools will it take to satisfy the hungry soul?

In his down-home style, Elder Jackson shares that as we behold the cross of Christ we will be ravished by His matchless charms. You will rejoice as you discover that, whether you have $2,700 or $27,000,000,000, Jesus is enough!

Enough for you and for me, for one and for all, for today and for eternity.

Hardcover • 128 Pages • ISBN 13: 978-0-8163-3790-3 • ISBN 10: 0-8163-3790-X

Pacific Press®
Publishing Association
"Where the Word Is Life"

Three ways to order:

1 Local | Adventist Book Center®
2 Call | 1-800-765-6955
3 Shop | AdventistBookCenter.com

 AdventistBookCenter.com   AdventistBookCenter   @AdventistBooks 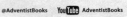 AdventistBooks